Walking
the Narrow
Path

*A 40-Day Journey to Finding Grace
and Unconditional Love*

ANITA STETTNER

BALBOA.PRESS
A DIVISION OF HAY HOUSE

Balboa Press books may be ordered through booksellers or by contacting:

Balboa Press
A Division of Hay House
1663 Liberty Drive
Bloomington, IN 47403
www.balboapress.com
844-682-1282

Because of the dynamic nature of the Internet, any web addresses or
links contained in this book may have changed since publication and
may no longer be valid. The views expressed in this work are solely those
of the author and do not necessarily reflect the views of the publisher,
and the publisher hereby disclaims any responsibility for them.

The author of this book does not dispense medical advice or prescribe
the use of any technique as a form of treatment for physical, emotional,
or medical problems without the advice of a physician, either directly
or indirectly. The intent of the author is only to offer information
of a general nature to help you in your quest for emotional and
spiritual well-being. In the event you use any of the information in
this book for yourself, which is your constitutional right, the author
and the publisher assume no responsibility for your actions.

Any people depicted in stock imagery provided by Getty Images are
models, and such images are being used for illustrative purposes only.
Certain stock imagery © Getty Images.

Print information available on the last page.

ISBN: 978-1-9822-5400-1 (sc)
ISBN: 978-1-9822-5401-8 (e)

Library of Congress Control Number: 2020916924

Balboa Press rev. date: 09/23/2020

Dedication

I lovingly dedicate this book to:

My Momsy, for teaching me to pray The Lord's Prayer and my bedtime prayers and bringing that routine into my life at such an early age. Thanks to you Jesus has always been present in my life, I do not know a life without Jesus.

My Dadsy, for being that continued reminder to walk the path of Jesus and to embrace our Christ-like qualities in all circumstances life presents.

My God Parents, for the spiritual guidance from my baptism through to this very day.

Because of their faith, guidance and wisdom I have been blessed with the presence of the Triune God in my life.

With Heartfelt Thanks

To my son, Dalton Derkson, editor extraordinaire, I am grateful for your craftsmanship and your ability to know what I am trying to say, then helping me find a better way to say it. Thank you for prompting me to dig deeper to provide more context for the readers. I appreciate the gentle nudging, encouragement and coaching along that way. You have always added so much light into my life, your ability to add humour to difficult situations and get mama to laugh is something I will treasure forever.

To my daughter, Bailee Johnson. You are my inspiration, you are the one who prompted me to make the healthy changes in my life. I am grateful to have such a lovely daughter who is my biggest cheerleader, confidante and best friend. I think, without even realizing it, you have always spoke truth into my life, which I will cherish forever.

To my inherited daughter, Brooklyn Langton. I prayed for you before I really knew you much and God placed you in my life in a way I would never have expected. You get me, thank you! I appreciate you jumping in and riding this journey with me. You and Huxley have been a precious addition to my family.

To my friends and family who have encouraged me on my journey - I love you all and I am who I am because of the wisdom, love and guidance you have all provided.

To my furry friends Kramer and Barney you were there the day I hit my rock bottom and let me know love does exist, I will be forever grateful for that inspirational encounter!

Contents

Introduction

Practicing a 40 day spiritual discipline is revolutionary and has the ability to change our relationship with ourselves, with others and with our environment. Spiritual discipline is deeply rooted in ancient times. The ability to bring your spiritual discipline practices into every moment of your daily routine allows you to have a connection of body, mind and soul. That connection will help to keep you fundamentally grounded when the chaos of this world tries to side swipe us and drag us into old patterns or habits.

I have found a 40 day spiritual discipline has helped me change unhealthy patterns in my life. When you are on a 40 day program you will notice healthy changes within 21 days and when you reach 40 days you have set a new healthy pattern in your life. The self improvement opportunities are endless, and from that, we learn to have healthier relationships with ourselves and with every circumstance we encounter on our life journey.

Healing can be found in the Light. Pure love is light. Fear, doubt and negativity is darkness. A spiritual disciple can bring light into the dark spaces if we participate. By participating we accept the invitation of the Spirit to dwell within us. One of my spiritual disciple favorites, Julie Clinton, says that we should be fearless knowing that: 'no darkness can withstand even the smallest light, so keep your hope candle burning.' (Be Fearless: Keep the Hope Candle Burning). When God stirs the heart we need to be willing to receive light and love to allow healing to take place. What does that feel like? I guess it is different for everyone. To me it is a heartfelt feeling that can rush (a wave of sensation) through your entire body. We will discuss this more as we move into the workings of the 40 day journey but just know it is a choice and we do need to accept and welcome the invitation.

At first, it is hard to pinpoint the internal stirrings but as you learn more about yourself you will begin to recognize your own body, mind, and soul cues. As we welcome the indwelling of the Spirit, we amp up the healing process. As we heal, there is still much darkness that surrounds us. Sadly, the cloak of darkness can be more appealing to us as we journey through our life, simply because it is comfortable. We might not like the darkness, but we are familiar with the darkness and until we are further into our healing journey the darkness will try and convince us to stay out of the Light which exists in each and every one of us. Choosing a spiritual discipline will let your light overcome the darkness and spark joy on your journey. Light shines in each one of us, and as we are able to get that light shining brighter, others will be able to recognize and be drawn to it. Imagine yourself becoming a lighthouse. Like moths to flames, others who seek the light knowingly or unknowingly become attracted to the light within you. The light isn't just healing to you it aids in the healing of others. As you heal yourself you are healing those closest to you, you are able to heal yourself and family from past trauma as well as set the healthy stage for future generations.

For me, using a 40 day spiritual discipline which embodies the entirety of our beings (that is our body, mind and soul) can produce beneficial self improvement results that can be further cultivated as we grow spiritually. Bringing that spiritual component into our healing allows us to centre ourselves developing our vertical (balanced) so that whatever is going on in the horizontal (imbalances) will not take us down. Developing a strong core mentally and physically allows one to be aligned with the source, our Creator, our God.

The 40 day spiritual discipline can be used as a prayer circle to petition for ourselves, to help others on their journey or for our entire community. As a prayer warrior, utilizing the 40 day prayer circle has allowed me to change my life and the world I live in one prayer at a time. 40 day prayer circles can help bring wisdom and God's direction into decisions or life circumstances. It is a valuable tool for any self care tool box.

The entire idea behind this book is that you do your best on this, your personal journey. You may need to start and restart a few times but I assure you that when you embrace this kind of healing, you will never let it go! The results for me and those I have worked with are amazing. I believe that healing starts on the inside then flows to our life patterns, I believe it takes heart, body, mind, soul and strength and I believe this 40 day program that brings together body, mind and soul will revolutionize your healing journey. What I have learned is self wellness is hard work! But very worth the effort.

I only know what I know, and I hope what I know will help you.

Being Spiritual

I shudder when people refer to me as religious. I prefer to be known as spiritual. My spiritual connection, my source of light is the triune God. My research and studies have opened my mind to the fact that we are all connected and wisdom from above is pure, peaceful and sincere. If your spiritual source has got any component attached to darkness or has a vibration of something other than that of kindness, peace and love then I encourage you to find a spiritual space that does spark joy.

I know a wise rancher that sits in his lawn chair at dawn with his cup of coffee looking and appreciating all the nature that surrounds him and says 'This is my church'. I respect that! This man may not be in church every Sunday or any Sunday, but he has a belief system that is pure, peaceful and sincere. He has found comfort in a space that is uplifting to his soul. He has slowed down and let go of the day to day struggles of ranching and farming and just sits. In that stillness he has engaged his senses. What he sees, hears, and smells brings him in to the present moment. Maybe a refreshing light wind blows on his face, or that first sip of coffee grabs his taste buds. He is comforted in the connection and relationship that he has with his 'church'. He has cultivated the ability to enjoy the peacefulness of nature and the love that established all of it. To have that place to worship the creation that surrounds him. To find that spot that speaks to his heart and stirs the spirit within him. We can all find that place of worship, that place that helps us ensure our anchors are set on a solid rock. To root us down and ground us in contentment and joy which allows us to rise up (or reset) and be the best versions of ourselves that we can be in any given moment in time.

My personal journey has led me to appreciate all that God created. For me, all I need is a sunset or sunrise to help me reset. To ensure my vertical (where my anchor is set) is connected to my Source of light. I assert that if our vertical (roots of our feet to crown of our head) is aligned, whatever is happening on the horizontal (the waves and winds of life) will not take us down or cause us to falter. I was raised Lutheran. I am a confirmed member of the Lutheran Church that is situated in the rough neighbourhood in which I was raised. As my pastor likes to say, we are a home for the 'black sheep'. What I have learned is the importance of finding that "church" which sparks joy and makes you feel at home. I drive over an hour back to my neighbourhood church to be with the other black sheep in my Christian family. I completely understand that church is not for everyone. I have been to plenty of churches that did not feel like home. I have helped many people on their own spiritual journey that turned away from the church because of the pain and hurt they personally experienced or their family experienced. Your church will be what stirs your heart and it will be a unique experience for you. What church does offer is community and a setting to worship with like minded people if that fits with your personal journey. In my life, where I am currently at, the community at my church has helped my spiritual growth just as much as sitting alone on a rock atop of a hill watching the sunset. Or listening to the neighbourhood woodpecker or squirrel or like my rancher friend sitting with a cup of coffee enjoying all that surrounds him. Finding that and leaning into that leads to spiritual growth uniquely and individually.

I am also fascinated by Indigenous spirituality and am very drawn to their teachings. The focus, appreciation and relationship to all the Creator has created (sacred and supernatural) while also connecting it to relationship with self and others has always sparked something in my soul. Whether or not my DNA is connected to that somehow or someway, my entire life I have been attracted to these beliefs and it has always stirred my heart. Assuredly the distant drumming that I remember hearing from our family cottage on First

Nations land or from that rock I sit on at top that big hill and hear the prairie chicken dance echo in the coulees, both have resonated with me and stirred my soul.

After my paternal grandmother passed I learned a great deal about Romanian Orthodox beliefs, rituals and icons. Sadly, it was after my grandmother died that I realized how connected my personal journey through my yoga training and the metaphysical encounters that I have experienced are so woven into the roots of my own ancestors.

Finding that spiritual connection that keeps you centered is personal work and has a great deal of personal choice. It is hard work, and takes an open mind to trying different approaches to see what resonates with who you are today. Remember that who you are today will evolve as you look for continuous personal growth.

Faith, hope and love are central to a solid spiritual connection. It is essential to have faith in what you believe. Again, wisdom is pure, peaceful and sincere so that our faith can be strong allowing us to believe, to have that spiritual connection. Hope is our anchor to our Source, our ability to check back with our Source and know we are secure so that doubt, worry and fear do not try and pull us away from our vertical. For me, I visualize that my vertical is an anchor firmly attached to a rock. That rock being the love of God. Love is the greatest gift of all. Love never fails and love is greater than fear. When we can cultivate our love connection, then our light truly shines. When our daily practice includes a self care technique that focuses on love of self, love of others and love of all creation we will have a solid foundation and building blocks in place for personal growth.

Self Care

Personal growth requires self care. In order to facilitate changes in our lives we need to give back to ourselves so that we can nourish our body, mind and soul. I assert that self care and our spirituality are key agents of changing unhealthy habits and patterns in our life. I encourage you to take time to investigate and journal about the things that nourish your body, mind and soul. Get to know who you are and what has either now or in the past sparked your joy. Being honest about who you are and what positive and negative patterns you have currently or from your past that tempt you.

Spending time alone, having quiet time built into your day will replenish the soul and help you learn more about who you are and where this journey is taking you. Being quiet is hard in a fast-paced society that expects things in an instant. This world and the people in it are demanding on our time and have a large chaotic component that is hard to resist as we have grown to accept the unacceptable. Self care involves setting healthy boundaries so that we are able to have the space in our lives to establish self care practices.

Self care helps us nourish our love of self, it helps us love others well and it also helps us love the nature that surrounds us. Meditation practices can be intimidating at first, they take time to establish and personalize. It is good to start small and try different ways of meditating until you find what is the best for your self care practice.

Meditation and breathing practices are both good ways to centre ourselves. Bringing the mind to the present moment and clearing the clutter of the mind so that the heart can do its healing work. The breath itself is so vital to our existence, it is pure nourishment to our body, mind and soul, yet we often fail to experience all that the breath can be and do within our body, mind and soul. Yoga has taught me just how powerful our breath is and can be. If we think about the importance of the breath when we help someone or ourselves out of the fight, flight or freeze state (panic attack), our breath is central to returning to the space of calm. We can train our bodies to focus on the breath, by taking deep cleansing breaths out of the belly over the front side of the heart. To help find that space of calmness, it is helpful to go through our 5 senses: 5 things we can see, 4 things we can feel, 3 things we can hear, 2 things we can smell and 1 thing we can taste. This allows us to get back to the calmness of the present moment. Our breath can help us when we are at an extreme (fight, flight or freeze state) or just needing to relax. A useful technique can be simply counting the breath or saying a short scripture or mantra that helps me calm the mind and focus on the breath flowing through my body. There are lots of styles of yogic breathing, prayer breath or meditation breathing, this is personal and we each will find what resonates best for our practice.

When our mind races we want to focus on clearing the clutter of the mind by allowing the breath to bring that mind space to the heart space. The heart space is a healing space. I assert that the seed of love is planted in each of our hearts and the heart also holds the Spirit of our Creator. This heart space — when cultivated, nurtured and cared for — will bloom in us and through us. I believe we have the capacity to heal ourselves from within as well as sparking others on their healing journey.

As life patterns cycle in unhealthy or dark places, *dis-ease* has the potential to harm you. *Dis-ease* is a holistic term referring to an imbalance within the body, it occurs when someone is out of alignment. Again, I assert this is when our vertical is not aligned to our Source or circumstances in our lives are not aligned causing us to cycle through patterns that are not life giving rather off putting causing the *dis-ease*. Much of the *dis-ease* that exists within our bodies due to our negative and unhealthy patterns. In time, this can be healed internally. *Dis-ease* attacks our adrenal glands, our joints, our ligaments and has the ability to lead to actual diseases and disabilities within our bodies, mind and soul. Self care brings the body back to a calm state where the healing (alignment) can begin.

A disciplined self care routine can be simple and fun. Some people pay lots of dollars to participate in self care programs or retreats while others can find self care options that are free and easily accessible. Whether the self care is guided or unguided, expensive or inexpensive, it all boils down to personal choice. Find what works best for your personal growth plan. In the Appendix section of this book I have provided helpful self care and meditation activities.

Appendix I - Self Soul Care Meditation
Appendix J - Centering Meditation
Appendix K - Camino Divina
Appendix L - Forest Bathing Meditation
Appendix M - Water Meditation
Appendix N - Gemstone Meditation
Appendix O - Seasonal Chakra Balancing - Sun Salutation Challenge
Appendix P - Chakra Prayer Meditation
Appendix Q - Grounding Meditation

Prayer and journaling are excellent self care activities in themselves or together. Having a daily routine that incorporates time for devotionals (or positive mantras), prayer and journaling will build stability into a healthy lifestyle. My own practice includes something I came across in both my yoga training and personal growth initiatives and it is called the "Daily Office." Peter Scazzero explains in Emotionally Healthy Relationships Day by Day: "It was about AD 525 when a monk named Benedict created a formal structure for these prayer times that he anchored in eight Daily Offices (including one for monks in the middle of the night). Prayer was the framework for the day, and everything else in their lives was ordered around it."

He goes on to explain that the "Daily Office" was key to creating a continual and easy familiarity with God's presence. I assert from my own experience that establishing a Daily Office routine in my life has led to much more success in assuring my vertical is anchored to my Source. In this way, when the winds of change blow through my life trying to rearrange my current circumstances, it is easier for me to bring myself back to the present moment and continue looking for the wisdom I need.

I recommend starting small with your daily self care routine. I started simply with a popular devotional that took less than 3 minutes, once a day. I would do this the moment I woke up, I got in the habit of having that devotional on my nightstand so that it was the first thing I grabbed in the morning. My day would end simply with a scripture reading or a simple prayer. This practice eventually grew. I discovered that having quiet time away from phones and social media is refreshing. I found that establishing a self care routine just had me crave more. My journaling practice took off and down the road I added nutritional components and body strengthening components. These practices changed for me as did the seasons of my life but as they changed so did I. My body wanted more self care which is pure restoration and such a healing ground. The miraculous thing is once you get to know your body more you will better understand what the body is asking you to do.

Nourishment

Fueling the vessel is vitally important to our overall wellness. Being mindful about the nourishing of our bodies will balance the body, mind and soul. This means having a healthy relationship with everything that goes into our body. The items we consume have the ability to heal us or the possibility of negatively affecting our body. Making mindful and wise choices about what we consume will help the body, mind and soul connection flourish.

When the body is cycling in negative and unhealthy patterns the typical result is unhealthy relationships with food, beverage, drugs, sex, others and self. Addiction is the most common way to soothe, mask or dull the pain of what is going on. Codependency is a common unhealthy relationship involving the self and others. My personal vice was codependency and not being able to find the exit out of abusive relationships. What I did not understand was that relationships do not take away from who we are. Rather, a healthy relationship adds to who we are and where we are going. Until I made the choice to change this unhealthy pattern I went from one abusive relationship straight into another. I know firsthand just how difficult it is to get out of that 'revolving door' and step out into the light. There were certainly times when fear had a death grip on me! In moments such as these, the abuser also tends to be a master manipulator. A puppet master in a way. So, the fear feels more real and can lower one's self-esteem. Paralyzing us, keeping us stuck in these situations.

When I look back on my journey and know what I know today about how the body can heal itself from the inside out, I am amazed at the process. Looking back on my personal journey and praying over what I have healed from and continue to learn from those experiences, has provided much clarity. That clarity with humbling honesty has identified several things: a.) I had a choice; b.) I was provided with opportunities; and c.) I had comfort which eventually helped me surrender.

As we gently surrender into the healing powers and do the slow and steady work of nourishing the body, mind and soul, the healing will begin. With a healthy relationship with nourishment we can begin to fuel our vessels with that which will allow personal growth.

I am not a fan of diet fads. I think they are set up for failure. I have found from my personal experience that eating according to the national food guide is the best option for everyone. Inasmuch as I recommend eating to the national food guide I will – depending on the specific situation – recommend elimination diets. Depending on your age and current health conditions it might be helpful to eliminate certain types of food or beverage.

For example, the average human being has sluggish bowels. This can be attributed to emotional stresses we carry in our body which can attack our digestive system. Our patterns of eating and drinking unhealthy amounts may cause physical abuse on our systems. It may be important to eliminate certain foods or liquids until our body reaches a steady state. Once we become mindfully aware of our bodies steady state we will be able to know and establish healthy eating habits.

Very early on in my journey I landed myself in the hospital, twice. Once with a blocked colon and once with acute back pain. Neither of these experiences were fun but I can look back at the progress I have made and find humour in both situations. Now the blocked colon was self induced. I went through a stage where cheesecake and milkshakes were my outlet for soothing the pain in my life. My system sent out a huge red flag and not only got my doctors attention but mine too. I was nudged in the direction of a healthy diet. The acute back pain is due to years of overworking, heavy lifting and rough sports. I worked in sales, logistics and business development and travelled extensively throughout my career, this included toting heavy luggage and lifting things in an unsafe manner. I have nerve damage in the lower back and bulging discs. When I was hospitalized for my acute back pain I was also 40 plus pounds overweight. After the hospital stay I was reintroduced to yoga as part of my physical therapy. I was also on the off ramp (unknowingly) of getting out of the final abusive relationship. I didn't know it then but I was on the road to recovery!

What I learned from both experiences is to listen to my body. Certain foods will send you messages, it is your choice if you lean in and learn or lean over and grab more. I realized that dairy did not work for my system. Especially the amount I was ingesting. As I welcomed new healthy habits I started researching more and discovered how gluten reacts in our body. Gluten causes inflammation therefore, those who suffer with stomach, back, hip or joint pain, eliminating or reducing gluten from their diet might find relief. I know I have as did those I have worked with.

I have learned that when my lower back pain shows up I need to look at what I have been eating. It was helpful to journal what I was eating to help me pinpoint where the sensitivity was. I do pride myself on eating healthy but I am human and sometimes my love of food gets the better of me. The solution for me is to be aware of the triggers and take an honest mindful assessment at what is the root cause of the flare up. Over doing any one thing will cause issues. Being mindful of portion size is an important aspect of the healing process.

Taking a mindful approach to shopping for and preparing foods will help you be grateful for the new healthy patterns. Learning and researching the benefits of different foods and their healing qualities is fascinating. My personal favorite is The Medical Medium, Anthony Williams. I recommend having a copy of "Life Changing Foods" in every household! The book is helpful to those who want to eat clean as well those of us that want to continue eating meat. It helps you know what food heals different ailments and what food helps remove toxins from the body. The biggest benefit from his book is once you have alignment in your life and you instinctively know what your body needs for nourishment, it is fun to see what spiritual lesson you might be learning or emotional trauma you might be healing. The truth is within us, we just have to be ready and willing to listen.

Water is essential. For most people it is difficult to consume the amount of water that is needed for our body on a daily basis. Some research indicates you can count all your liquids consumed and not just water. I am not certain I can completely agree. While yes, coffee, soda and alcoholic beverages are definitely liquids we consume, they do have negative attributes in which they carry with the benefit of being a liquid. I have found that some liquids will dehydrate instead of hydrate the body. For me, each night I prepare a 16 oz glass of water with several lemon slices so that the first thing I drink in the morning is 16 oz of lemon water. Lemon water prepares our body for the day. It is an alkali as it enters the body and has helped my complexion, my regularity and brightens my day. Throughout my day I drink hot lemon water and sometimes even add a little rosehip hibiscus tea to sweeten my day. The hot lemon water helps kill harmful bacteria or viruses trying to get into your body and rosehip has been known to help upper respiratory and helps with inflammation in our body.

The Medical Medium speaks about lemon water and that it is excellent for the immune system, detoxifying the liver and body, rehydrating, and even helping with nausea. He too suggests lemon water every morning first thing and suggests to make more to drink throughout the day.

It certainly was a transition for me to switch my liquid intake from things like soda pop to a healthier alternative. For me I set a goal to allow only one Pepsi per month. This goal was noted on my calendar in the kitchen for everyone to see and keep me honest. There is something about putting goals on a calendar and making it public, it kinda keeps a person accountable. It was a struggle with significant rewards in the end. Eliminating processed sugars found in soda pop and replacing them with healthier alternatives allowed me to catapult into a healthier leaner me. For me the replacement was sparkling mineral water or club soda. Even by adding just a slice of lemon or lime helped add flavor to the bubbles. Fast forwarding this achievement into today I now find it unbearable to drink those types of liquids. Was it easy, heck no! But keeping to a goal and being honest and accountable through the process was an epic adventure. Being accountable came with rewards too. My kids were my accountability coaches, they would award me an extra cola on a special holiday or Super Bowl Sunday.

Club Soda or sparkling mineral water is a good substitution for soda pop, there are so many flavours or you can just add a fresh lemon or lime slice. I encourage you to find a healthy relationship to water (bubbly or still). It has an amazing effect on the healing of your body, mind and soul.

You can also nourish the body with good vibrations. Music can have a positive healing effect on the body, mind and soul. Sound vibrations have a metaphysical ability to heal our bodies. Spoken words of high vibration have the ability to heal our bodies from the inside out. Think about that song that raises your consciousness, grabs your body, mind and soul. It might be different songs in different seasons of your journey, but it is worth paying attention to what these songs stir in your innermost being. When a song or spoken words can spark joy, I encourage you to pay attention and lean into it. Welcome and become aware of the body, mind, soul connection. Dive in and explore the emotions it creates. As we accept the invitation to lean in, the healing begins. God truly uses music to move us, to connect us with himself, with others and with ourselves.

Having a better understanding of the chakras (energy centres in the body) and how they work and how they can facilitate healing within the body will open up another dynamic in your journey. These chakras are described as wheels at distinct points within the body. If energy in the body is not flowing efficiently the chakras are said to become 'stuck'. When there is *disease* in the body it is believed that the wheels have been stuck or not effectively flowing energy. These chakras are sensitive to different sounds and tones, Once your chakras are aligned you become more keen, alert and aware of body sensations. When we have the ability to feed that sensation it leads to healing the entire body. My own personal discovery has led me to identify that different tones are more keenly sensed at the different chakras. For example different pitches and tones relate to each chakra. Being mindfully aware of the chakras allow for heightened sensuality to healing vibrations.

Good vibrations can also come from the energy produced around like-minded people or people you feel comfortable and safe with. Place yourself in the centre of good energy and your body will be nourished.

Gemstones have miraculous nourishing powers. I was reluctant to believe that rocks carried vibrations.... until that one day when I knew they did. Since I can remember, I was always drawn to rocks and gemstones. I owned a store and sold rocks and gemstones for years before I realized the powerful healing vibrations gemstones held. There is so much to learn and I feel like my learning has just begun. From my personal experience, I started with laying rose quartz on my chest as I settled in for my nightly devotions and prayers. Something just called me to do this. Rose quartz was so calming and gentle. It helped me focus on love of self. It helped me centre my heart space and bring me peace. Similarly, when I started meditating on a regular basis I would hold chrysoprase in my hands. It would let me feel things in a comforting and safe way. It allowed me to dive into the emotion to learn from it and in that safe place to let it go. As I let those feelings go I would have a calming cleansed feeling after my meditation. I assert that the rock picks you, you do not pick the rock. It is a scientific fact that gemstones have vibrations, they have stored energy. Healing energy! The healing energy that only God could create. You will either believe it or you won't, but if you do find yourself drawn to gemstones, I encourage you to lean into the healing available. I have included a gemstone prayer meditation within the appendix of this book.

Appendix N - Gemstone Meditation

I do encourage you to always check facts on anything that challenges your personal beliefs. If something is challenging, take it up with God. He will ensure all things align with your vertical.

Each evening there will be a journal prompt where you can record or write about the nourishment for that day.

Movement

Yoga is the unification of meditation, breath works and movement. Yoga has been the ultimate cure for my healing journey. The moment you can bring all three of those together it is like the best medicine ever! Meditation brings the mind space to the heart space. The yogic breathing takes the healing breath throughout the body and while we move we are activating the chakras, the meridian lines, the glandular, digestive, reproductive and nervous systems. The chakras run up the spine while the meridian lines run through the organs in our body. These are like energy systems that are important to keep healthy for the entirety of our beings.

As we move, we breathe. As we breathe we inhale healing and as we exhale it is a two- part sensation. We let go of all that is no longer needed and we allow the healing breath to flow throughout the body. If you can visualize that breathe as it flows through your body, pay attention to where it might be getting held up or sticky. Focus on those areas and visualize the breath breaking down the barriers, the strongholds, the stress and let the healing into those areas.

When you can bring the union of meditation, breath work and movement into your entire exercise routine you will notice a big improvement. Walking in itself is a wonderful exercise for the body, mind and soul. If you can bring the mindfulness and breathing into the mix, you can really kick it up a notch. A couple summers ago I volunteered at an outreach event. I was partnered up with a retired couple. One was a doctor the other a pharmacist, we discussed different treatments for depression and the doctor said he always prescribes walking for depression. When we can "keep on keeping on" we can move from that place of darkness or depression into the light where healing can happen. Simply walking mindfully is a great start.

Dancing is a great way to get unstuck. Dancing as a group or dancing alone in your pajamas in your living room with your boots on is what I do. Dancing is movement. When we can get to shaking those hips or shoulders we are providing healing to the chakras, the meridian lines and the adrenal glands. I find it to be an instant mood changer and energy sparkler that dynamically changes the energy flow in the body, which enhances the inner and outer beauty of the movement.

For my personal journey it was helpful for me to journal about my movement. What I did and how it made me feel and what things it might have brought up. Each day you will have a journal prompt where you can list or write about your movement throughout the day.

Let the Journey Begin!

As you enter into a 40 day journey to deeply heal or make positive changes in your life it is important to establish your starting point and set some intentions for the journey. It starts with allowing grace to be the foundation of this practice. Being diligent with a practice that dislodges old habits and roots down new healthy habits requires much grace. You might not make it the full 40 days the first time you try, that is okay! Let grace allow you to restart. Sometimes when I go through a 40 day set program I might find something that is speaking to my soul and I might want to hover over that day for a few days or a week and let it soak in longer. Have grace with yourself, all the while acknowledging and journaling about your inner discoveries.

The 40 day practice is meant to declutter the mind and spark joy in your heart, allowing peace to settle into your entire day. Sometimes the mind or the ego will make you overthink and you might question whether or not you are getting the practice right. If that happens, just bring it back to your breath and find grace in the present moment. This practice is *your* personal journey with guideposts. Whatever you are doing, you are doing it right. Overthinking gets you into your head space and we want to get out of that head space and let the heart space take over and send a calming feeling throughout the body. Just remember, if the mind tries to take over, give yourself grace to allow that breath to bring the mind space to the heart space. Every fresh breath and step you take on your wellness journey is forward momentum.

For me it is a natural at home feeling, a peaceful feeling when I can plug into my Source and allow the restoration to take place when I am doing my Daily Office. While this is a deliberate routine in my life now, it has not always been that way. My 40 day journeys have taken on different shapes over the seasons of my life and it has evolved into the form in which they hold today. When I started it was not easy and took hard work and some restarts. That peaceful feeling was not always there and, for a large part of my life (through my personal struggles, traumas) I was not at peace. I had lost my spiritual connection as my life choices took a toll on me, my body, mind and soul. Life got so bad for me because of my choices. I believed the voices in my head and the voice of the manipulative narcissistic partner. I had no self worth; I was unhealthy in every imaginable way before I made the choice and the effort to make positive changes in my life.

It all comes to personal choice. Being joyful is a choice. Being thankful and grateful are choices we make to appreciate ourselves, our God, other things or other people. Loving ourselves, others and all of God's creation is a personal choice. You have picked up this book as a choice and I am prayerfully hopeful you can pick up a nugget or two to help you on your journey.

What to Expect

I believe wholeheartedly that a 40 day spiritual disciple is entirely enriching and healing. By leaning on the expertise of those who helped me through to where I stand today I have created a guide for which I hope helps you. The guide I have shared here is built from my own experience and success with a 40 day journey.

You'll find plenty of research on the effectiveness of 40 day programs or treatments. It is a long held spiritual belief that a period of 40 days allows you time to break a habit then lay down the foundation of a healthy, new pattern. It is the consistency over time that allows us to reprogram our body, mind and soul. It also requires the dedication, commitment and patience with the process. Each 40 day journey I have tried has brought me closer to God and allowed me a deeper appreciation of my own spiritual growth. My two most significant and powerful 40 day journeys have actually been during the season of Lent. Based on those powerful experiences I have divided this 40 day journey into 8 segments:

Love of self
Kindness, peace and love blooming
Fruits of the Spirit

Going back to go forward
Listening
Restoring
Growing
Walking the narrow path

Each segment will have a theme which we will explore for 5 days.

Each day will have elements of:
Silence, stillness and centering
Devotional reading
Journal thoughts, questions or observations
Nourishment
Movement
Prayer

<u>Silence, stillness and centering:</u> This is your mindfulness training. It is important to take a minimum of 2 minutes each morning and night just for silence. Then, another 2-3 minutes to meditate on three specific phrases. Meditation has wonderful total body benefits. There is much research that supports the importance of a daily meditation practice. Finding that sacred silence is an important component during a meditation practice. My personal practice grew dynamically when I started practicing sacred silence during Lent. We have a basic need for spiritual

fulfilment, centering prayer, silence and stillness facilitates that growth. I value the work of Dr. Caroline Leaf who says 'Intense prayer and meditation change numerous structures and functions in the brain, thus changing the way you perceive reality.' By taking time to slow down the brain and declutter the thoughts, we can have a healthier view on reality and make better choices. Some people are wonderful at meditation - it comes easy to them. For others, it is work in progress. This is *your* personal practice, feel free to meditate longer if you are more comfortable with it. I have noted from my own experiences and from those of my clients that daily meditation supplemented with one longer meditation session per week does wonders for the brain.

Devotional reading: The selected readings will provide guidance, wisdom and knowledge. Loving God and receiving God's love is at our own disposal. It is a choice. We just need to accept the invitation given by the reading and open the ears of our heart. Something that has helped me grow spiritually is opening the ears of the heart. Opening those ears was not easy at first, I found by just simply saying 'Holy Spirit you are welcome here' before I would read something was invitation enough.

<u>Journal thoughts, questions or observations:</u> After the reading, prayerfully write what stuck out for you in the text. There will be journal prompts provided each day to help you let the pen flow. If you are not big into journaling, let this serve as a learning exercise for you. Be patient and have grace for whatever you are able to do. Some people write like mad, others doodle their ideas, some like bullet journaling. This is your practice, find what is comfortable for you. It is good brainwork to read over what you wrote. I also sometimes like going back to what I wrote in the morning so I know what prayers I need to be thankful for later on, or how God moved mountains in my day.

<u>Nourishment:</u> Each morning and night there will be a prompt to drink lemon water. Not only is hydration important but I have found through my own journey the benefit of this practice. This helps balance our systems to help with constipation, inflammation and complexion (just to name a few benefits). It has worked wonders in my life as well as the lives of those I have coached or mentored. There will be journal prompts where you can briefly list your daily nourishment. When I was doing elimination diets or fasting, this was an important element of my daily practice. Journal what feels right for your practice.

<u>Movement:</u> Movement is so important for the body, mind and soul. I will recommend restorative yoga poses each day for the silence, stillness and centering exercise. There will be yoga flows and other exercise routines listed in the Appendix. There will also be a daily journal prompt where you can note your steps, distance travelled or other workout information.

Appendix R - Yoga Sequences

<u>Prayer:</u> Each morning I will provide a morning prayer. Each evening you can come up with your own prayer. You might choose to do journal prayers. You might have a specific prayer or scripture that has significance in your life. In the appendix I have provided additional prayers for morning, evenings and prayers for other people or situations you may be up against. Praying may come easy to you or it might be hard. Be patient with yourself and grow your prayer life. I am finally getting better at knowing what it is like to pray without ceasing. Even though I still have lots to learn!

Appendix A - The Lord's Prayer
Appendix B - Placing the Cross Prayer
Appendix C - Praying for Children
Appendix D - Praying for Friend or Family Member
Appendix E - Selection of Morning Prayers
Appendix F - Selection of Evening Prayers

SEGMENT 1

～

Love of Self – A practice of self discovery

The practice of self discovery allows us to get to know ourselves from the inside out. I have found that healing is an inside job. We heal ourselves from the inside out. Our first step is taking an honest look at what is inside.

The second step is letting Our Creator inside. Letting love inside. That tenderness of lovingkindness allows the healing to start. It is a choice which each of us have to make. This inside healing job is not easy work and it is certainly not clean work. But it is worth the work!

1 John 4:16 and 19 The Voice

We have experienced and we have entrusted our lives to the love of God in us. God is love. Anyone who lives faithfully in love also lives faithfully in God, and God lives in him.

We love because he first loved us.

As we accept the invitation to allow love in, the Spirit of love is like an ointment that will supercharge our body, mind and soul.

Day 1 Morning

Find a comfortable restorative pose, one hand on heart one hand on belly recognizing the breath as it flows through the body. Enjoy the silence and calmness for at least 2 minutes, paying attention to the breath, the gentle rise and fall of the chest and belly.

Silence, stillness and centering for a minimum of 2 minutes on:
I am loved, I am loving, I am loveable.

Devotional reading:

Lamentations 3:19-30 The Message

I'll never forget the trouble, the utter lostness,
    the taste of ashes, the poison I've swallowed.
I remember it all – oh, how I remember –
    the feeling of hitting the bottom.
But there's one other thing I remember,
    and remembering, I keep a grip on hope;

God's loyal love couldn't have run out,
    his merciful love couldn't have dried up.

They're created new every morning.
>   How great your faithfulness!
I'm sticking with God (I say it over and over).
>   He's all I've got left.

God proves to be good to the man who passionately
waits, to the woman who diligently seeks.
It's good thing to quietly hope,
>   quietly hope for help from God…

When life is heavy and hard to take,
>   Go off by yourself. Enter silence.
Bow in prayer. Don't ask questions:
>   Wait for hope to appear.
Don't run from trouble. Take it full-face.
>   The 'worst' is never the worst.

This quote from Lamentations reminds us that when
we find ourselves in even the darkest moments of our
lives, there is still hope. When life gets 'heavy and
hard to take' have the personal diligence to go off by
yourself. Find silence and solitude. Pray and don't ask
questions. Don't run away or find a way to mask the
issue. Take it on, dive into the emotion, hand it over to
God — the Source of your being — and patiently wait
for hope to appear.

Journal Prompts:

What came up for you while reading this verse? What intentions are you setting for yourself today? What will you take forward and think about today?

Morning Prayer:

May I walk humbly today knowing I am loved, that I am loving and I am truly loveable. Amen.

Nourishment:

Enjoy a cup of lemon water to prepare your body for the day.

Movement:

Standing in Mountain Position, interlace your fingers behind your back. Roll the shoulders to the back body and tilt the chin to the ceiling. Take three cleansing breaths over the front side of the heart. This allows the tension to roll off our shoulders while opening the heart and throat chakras.

Day 1 Evening

Nourishment:

Enjoying a cup of hot lemon water to help slow your body and mind down for restoration.

Slowing the movement:

From a comfortable reclined restorative position, place both hands on the belly. Recognize the rise and fall of the breath. Relax in silence for a minimum of 2 minutes.

Silence, stillness and centering on:
I am loved, I am loving, I am loveable.

Devotional reading:

You have been asked to do only this:

To act justly;
To love mercy;
and to walk humbly.

(adapted from Micah 6:8 Tree of Life)

Journal:

Reviewing your day, how have you been able to act justly, to love mercy and walk humbly? Do a personal inventory of areas of self improvement on your day. Journal those things you are thankful for and things you remain hopeful of.

Additional journal prompts for overall health and wellness:
~nourishment
~movement

Pray.

Day 2 Morning

Find a comfortable restorative pose, one hand on heart one hand on belly recognizing the breath as it flows through the body. Enjoy the silence and calmness for at least 2 minutes, paying attention to the breath, the gentle rise and fall of the chest and belly.

Silence, stillness and centering for a minimum of 2 minutes on:
I am loved, I am loving, I am loveable.

Devotional reading:

Often it is helpful to look at a scripture from different translations. Sometimes one translation will stir your heart more than another. As we look at James 3:17-18 which of these four translations stirs your heart the most?

God's Word

> ...the wisdom that comes from above is first of all pure. Then it is peaceful, gentle, obedient, filled with mercy and good deeds, impartial, and sincere. The harvest that has God's approval comes from the peace planted by peacemakers.

The Living Bible

> ...the wisdom that comes from heaven is first of all pure and full of quiet gentleness. Then it is peace-loving and courteous. It allows discussion and is willing to yield to others; it is full of mercy and good deeds. It is wholehearted and straightforward and sincere. And those who are peacemakers will plant seeds of peace and reap a harvest of goodness.

The Voice

> Heavenly wisdom centers on purity, peace, gentleness, deference, mercy, and other good fruits untainted by hypocrisy. The seed that flowers into righteousness will always be planted in peace by those who embrace peace.

The Passion

> ...the wisdom from above is always pure, filled with peace, considerate and teachable. It is filled with love and never displays prejudice or hypocrisy in any form and it always bears the beautiful harvest of righteousness! Good seeds of wisdom's fruit will be planted with peaceful acts by those who cherish making peace.

I love how The Passion ends this scripture. To me this means that for those walking like Jesus, those who live each day in peace, good seeds will grow. It also talks about wisdom from heaven being "considerate and teachable." I find that inspirational. Good seeds of wisdom's fruit are planted so that they grow and in a gentle way nudges us to a teachable moment. If we accept the Holy Spirit's invitation to provide us with teachable wisdom however the chaotic lives we lead sometimes have us marching to our own beat.

The Voice says, 'The seed that flowers into righteousness will always be planted in peace by those who embrace peace.' It also states wisdom centers on "purity and deference." Deference was a new concept for me, it involves humble submission and respect. Submission and respect to the Spirit of God within us or how the Spirit has placed the wisdom before us.

If we can focus our attention away from jealousy and selfish ambition we can avoid chaos and negative energies looming in our lives. Therefore, if we focus on what is purely peaceful and sincere, our mind will be aligned to our vertical which is anchored to our Source. It allows us to centre ourselves so that we can rise up and endure the chaos and negativity that we face day to day.

Journal:

What came up for you while reading this verse? What intentions are you setting for yourself today? What will you take forward and think about today?

Morning Prayer:

God, grant me the serenity to accept the things I cannot change, courage to change the things that I can and wisdom to know the difference.

Nourishment:

Enjoy a cup of lemon water to prepare your body for the day.

Movement:

Standing in Mountain Position, interlace your fingers behind your back. Roll the shoulders to the back body and tilt the chin to the ceiling. Taking three cleansing breaths over the front side of the heart. This allows the tension to roll off our shoulders while opening the heart and throat chakras.

Day 2 Evening

Nourishment:

Enjoying a cup of hot lemon water to help slow your body and mind down for restoration.

Slowing the movement:

From a comfortable reclined restorative position, place both hands on the belly. Recognize the rise and fall of the breath. Relax in silence for a minimum of 2 minutes.

Silence, stillness and centering on:
I am loved, I am loving, I am loveable.

Devotional reading:

James 3:13-18 The Message

Live Well, Live Wisely

Do you want to be counted wise, to build a reputation for wisdom? Here's what you do: Live well, live wisely, live humbly. It's the way you live, not the way you talk, that counts. Mean spirited ambition isn't wisdom. Boasting that you are wise isn't wisdom. Twisting the truth to make yourselves sound wise isn't wisdom. It is the furthest thing from wisdom – it's animal cunning, devilish conniving. Whenever you're trying to look better of others, things fall apart and everyone ends up at the others' throats.

Real wisdom, God's wisdom, begins with a holy life and is characterized by getting along with others. It is gentle and reasonable, overflowing with mercy and blessings, not hot one day and cold the next, not two-faced. You can develop a healthy, robust community that lives right with God and enjoy its results only if you do the hard work of getting along with each other, treating each other with dignity and honor.

The Message translation offers practical what is and is not wisdom. Emphasizing that 'real wisdom, God's wisdom' is consistent and overflows with mercy and blessings. Walking in God's wisdom each and every day is not an easy task. Self improvement exercises are not easy work. They are hard work. Pat your back for getting started on the hard work that comes from establishing order in your life. By aligning your vertical so that the horizontal doesn't drag you into chaos and unhealthy patterns.

Journal:

Reviewing your day, how have you lived well, lived wisely, lived humbly? Self examine where you could have leaned in more to God. What are you nailing to the cross today? Journal those things you are thankful for and things you remain hopeful of.

Additional journal prompts for overall health and wellness:
~nourishment
~movement

Pray.

Day 3 Morning

Find a comfortable restorative pose, one hand on heart one hand on belly recognizing the breath as it flows through the body. Enjoy the silence and calmness for at least 2 minutes, paying attention to the breath, the gentle rise and fall of the chest and belly.

Silence, stillness and centering for a minimum of 2 minutes on:
I am loved, I am loving, I am loveable.

Devotional reading:

Solitude and prayer allows for a direct connection to our Source. It allows us to stay connected to the vertical when things on the horizontal start distracting us. Prayer nourishes the soul and when the soul is nourished we can better love ourselves and we can see the love of God in others.

Psalm 62:5-8 Christian Standard

Rest in God alone, my soul, for my hope comes from him. He alone is my rock and my salvation, my stronghold; I will not be shaken. My salvation and glory depend on God, my strong rock. My refuge is in God. Trust in him at all times, you people; pour out your hearts before him.

Through quiet contemplation we can centre ourselves in the restoration of God's love. As we open up our hearts to him in silence he will nourish our souls with his soft whispers in and through us. Once we are able to present ourselves to the Lord in stillness, calmness and wait on Him, it is a far easier task for him to create a pure heart in us.

Journal:

What came up for you while reading this verse? What intentions are you setting for yourself today? How can you make this a reality in your life today?

Morning Prayer:

I arise today through the strength of heaven;
    Light of sun, radiance of moon,
    Splendor of fire; speed of lightning,
    Swiftness of wind, depth of sea,
    Stability of earth, firmness of rock.
I arise today through God's strength to pilot me...
    God's word to speak for me,
    God's hand to guard me,
    God's way to lie before me...
I summon today all these powers between me and evil,
    Against every cruel, merciless power that
    may oppose my body and soul.

- Attributed to Saint Patrick, 500 AD

Nourishment:

Enjoy a cup of lemon water to prepare your body for the day.

Movement:

Standing in Mountain Position, interlace your fingers behind your back. Roll the shoulders to the back body and tilt the chin to the ceiling. Take three cleansing breaths over the front side of the heart. This allows the tension to roll off our shoulders while opening the heart and throat chakras.

Day 3 Evening

Nourishment:

Enjoying a cup of hot lemon water to help slow your body and mind down for restoration.

Slowing the movement:

From a comfortable reclined restorative position, place both hands on the belly. Recognize the rise and fall of the breath. Relax in silence for a minimum of 2 minutes.

Silence, stillness and centering on:
I am loved, I am loving, I am loveable.

Devotional:

1 Peter 5:7 NASB

Cast all your anxiety on Him, because He cares for you.

When we cast our anxiety on Him, our Source, our Creator, we create a space for healing. When we can be honest with ourselves and honest with our God who knows all, we create a space to let God in and heal our broken bits. It is a choice and a positive step toward being honest with ourselves and loving ourselves exactly where we are.

Journal:

Reviewing your day, have you been able to cast all your anxiety on Him? What is holding you back from casting all your anxiety on Him? Self examine where you could have leaned in more to God. Journal those things you are thankful for and things you remain hopeful of.

Additional journal prompts for overall health and wellness:
~nourishment
~movement

Pray.

Day 4 Morning

Find a comfortable restorative pose, one hand on heart one hand on belly recognizing the breath as it flows through the body. Enjoy the silence and calmness for at least 2 minutes, paying attention to the breath, the gentle rise and fall of the chest and belly.

Silence, stillness and centering for a minimum of 2 minutes on:
I am loved, I am loving, I am loveable.

Devotional reading:

Each time a rainbow appears, stretching from one end of the sky to the other, it's God renewing His promise. Each shade of color, each facet of light displays the radiant spectrum of God's love – a promise that life can be new for each one of us.

- Wendy Moore

This beautiful quote brings to mind a favorite scripture that I often read as the mediation verse for my yoga classes. Taken from The Message (God)...rekindles burned-out lives with fresh hope, restoring dignity and respect to their lives - a place (truly) in the sun!

A rainbow does just that, a spectrum of God's love on display and for me in my life the rainbow gives me that pause to be patient with myself, my life, my circumstances and just breath in God's love that gives us so much hope.

Journal:

What came up for you while reading this verse? What new things are you looking forward to today? What intentions are you setting for yourself today? Where can you find the radiant spectrum of God's love today?

Morning Prayer:

May I see your promises today. May I see your beauty which surrounds me. Amen.

Nourishment:

Enjoy a cup of lemon water to prepare your body for the day.

Movement:

Standing in Mountain Position, interlace your fingers behind your back. Roll the shoulders to the back body and tilt the chin to the ceiling. Take three cleansing breaths over the front side of the heart. This allows the tension to roll off our shoulders while opening the heart and throat chakras.

Day 4 Evening

Nourishment:

Enjoying a cup of hot lemon water to help slow your body and mind down for restoration.

Movement:

From a comfortable reclined restorative position, place both hands on the belly. Recognize the rise and fall of the breath. Relax in silence for a minimum of 2 minutes.

Silence, stillness and centering on:
I am loved, I am loving, I am loveable.

Devotional:

As we study Psalm 145:13 we will look at it from two translations. As we think about the spectrum of God's love for each of us and developing our trust, faith and hope in Him and thinking how we can live our lives in a space of love, notice what stirs your heart with these two translations:

NIV

The Lord is trustworthy in all he promises
and faithful in all he does.

The Passion

You are faithful to fulfill every promise you've made.
You manifest yourself as kindness in all you do.

Journal:

Reviewing your day, where has your faith stood strong?
Where could you have leaned more into faith today?
Journal those things you are thankful for and things
you remain hopeful of.

Additional journal prompts for overall health and wellness:
~nourishment
~movement

Pray.

Day 5 Morning

Find a comfortable restorative pose, one hand on heart
one hand on belly recognizing the breath as it flows
through the body. Enjoy the silence and calmness for

at least 2 minutes, paying attention to the breath, the gentle rise and fall of the chest and belly.

Silence, stillness and centering for a minimum of 2 minutes on:
I am loved, I am loving, I am loveable.

Devotional reading:

The Apostle Paul writes to Titus:

> It's true that all is pure to those who have pure hearts. (Titus 1:15 The Passion)

Thomas Keaton in *The Heart of the World* discusses:

> "Humility of heart is not only just to be. It is also the spontaneous capacity just to do. One cannot just do until he has first learned just to be. It is out of that experience of just being that one can then be content with the joy of just doing. Just doing doesn't mean that one does not have a purpose, does not think, does not plan. But in imposing one's will and intentions on reality and on events, one does not lose basic experience and joy of just doing. As a child retains joy of just seeing as it learns to distinguish between the various things that it sees, so we must be able to do without losing the capacity to judge. Our problem is that we get

wrapped up in what we are doing and why we are doing it – analyzing it, planning, worrying about it – so that we lose the joy that is always available – of just doing.

Just to be, just to do – these are the two great gifts of God, the foundations of every other gift. We need to return to these two great capacities again and again cultivate them. The events of daily life need to be placed in perspective by a deep sense of prayer, by learning how to be before God. Then, as reality comes in upon us, we will perceive each event as the working of the Holy Spirit, carefully designed for our particular needs. Every event is a touch of the living finger of God, which is sketching in us – body, soul and spirit – the true image of his Son, the being that the Father originally gave us and which he is restoring.

…Accepting that gift is accepting God's will for us, and in its acceptance lies the path to growth and ultimate fulfillment."

It is so easy to get caught in the doing. I know I am guilty of analyzing and worrying about the how and the why. It is a human response that can be gently guided into a space of contemplation. Accepting the invitation and placing your worries and fears before

God. This allows you to create a space for His wisdom to flow into your reality.

Journal:

What came up for you while reading this verse? Are you comfortable or uncomfortable with the concept of: 'just to be, just to do'? What intentions are you setting for today to not get wrapped up in 'doing'? What will you take forward and think about today?

Morning Prayer:

Lord help me just be in your presence today. Amen.

Nourishment:

Enjoy a cup of lemon water to prepare your body for the day.

Movement:

Standing in Mountain Position, interlace your fingers behind your back. Roll the shoulders to the back body and tilt the chin to the ceiling. Take three cleansing breaths over the front side of the heart. This allows the tension to roll off our shoulders while opening the heart and throat chakras.

Day 5 Evening

Nourishment:

Enjoying a cup of hot lemon water to help slow your body and mind down for restoration.

Movement:

From a comfortable reclined restorative position, place both hands on the belly. Recognize the rise and fall of the breath. Relax in silence for a minimum of 2 minutes.

Silence, stillness and centering on:
I am loved, I am loving, I am loveable.

Devotional:

1 Thessalonians 5:16-18 TLB

Always be joyful. Always keep on praying. No matter what happens, always be thankful, for this is God's will for you.

This scripture reminds us to be content in any and all situations. I find that when my mind tries to step in and take charge of a circumstance to which I am faced with, I send up a quick prayer or I quickly say "Lord have mercy, Christ have mercy" over and over to get my mind back to being captive in the heart space so that the joy fills my heart no matter how difficult the situation is. It is helpful to even ask God or the Holy Spirit to show you the joy if you can't immediately recognize it. I've often cried out in prayer 'Lord I need to see where you are in this circumstance'. Learning how you speak with God and how He or the Spirit speaks to you is the act of accepting His invitation into your heart.

Journal:

Reviewing your day, list the joyful moments you encountered, list the blessings you are thankful for. Self examine where you could have leaned more into His love today.

Pray.

Throughout this Segment - Love of Self, we did a self discovery. We took an honest look at ourselves and we accepted the invitation to let God in so that we can open ourselves up for radical transformation. Stirring up that heart and letting love in, embracing God's love heart and soul ignites the healing process. God is love. When we take up permanent residence in a life of love, we live in God and God lives in us. This way, love has the run of the house, becomes at home and mature in us, so that we're free of worry...there is no room in love for fear. Well formed love banishes fear. We are going to love, love and be loved. First we were loved, now we love. He loved us first. (1 John 1:16-19) We are relational creatures. We are wired to have intimate relationships with God, ourselves and others.

SEGMENT 2

~

Love Blooming

The greatest gift is love! When we invite love in and embrace it, love starts to bloom both in us and from us. When we take on the attitude of loving like our lives depended on it, we see significant growth and healing in our body, mind and soul.

Our body, mind and souls are wired to live in that space of love. We were born to love. Yet, as we grow up we learn to fear, worry and doubt our ways through the things we come up against in our lives. Once we recognize and accept the invitation of the Holy Spirit, we can start to retrain our body, mind and souls in the language of love. In that way we can heal ourselves and those who God places in our lives.

I believe that once we get that heart chakra "spinning" or "glowing" — essentially getting that energy moving — the heart chakra has the ability to spark the other chakras and start the flow of healing energy. It is truly a dedicated exercise of body, mind and soul to continuously bring things back to love. This is where the cleansing breath is helpful. Concentrating on getting a big enough breath out of the belly over the front side of the heart. So big a breath that you are able to capture the mind space and bring it back to the heart space is the essence of bringing it back to love. Having that calming, thoughtful, and peaceful sensation that is felt when the thoughts are cultivated within the space of the heart. So then, if we bring it back to love, we can begin to establish that love is greater than fear. When fear or doubt kicks in we can use the breath to bring those thoughts captive to the heart. As we get better at this exercise of bringing things to the healing space of the heart, we can then experience the realization that love never fails. It is a healthy circular flow of loving energy from the heart to the brain so that the brain can declutter and be refreshed. So if we put our faith in love and what it is meant to be in our lives (a loving heart), our entire bodies will benefit. Living a heart centred life will allow love to blossom in and through you.

Day 1 Morning

Find a comfortable restorative pose, one hand on heart one hand on belly recognizing the breath as it flows through the body. Enjoy the silence and calmness for at least 2 minutes, paying attention to the breath, the gentle rise and fall of the chest and belly.

Silence, stillness and centering for a minimum of 2 minutes on:

I have faith, I have hope, I have love.

Devotional reading:

Jude 1:2 – The Message

Relax, everything's going to be alright; rest, everything's coming together; open your hearts, love is on the way!

This quote from Jude reminds us that everything is going to work out. We need to open our hearts and let love bloom. By first opening our hearts to love, we can then allow the love to bloom in us and through us. Think of it as a seed planted in our heart space. If we open that heart space up and allow love in, the seed will grow and give us the courage and strength to love ourselves and those who are placed in our lives.

Journal:

What came up for you while reading this devotion? What intentions are you setting for yourself today? As you go through your day pay attention to what stirs your heart.

Morning Prayer:

May I walk with confidence and may I walk in the wake of love. Amen.

Nourishment:

Enjoy a cup of lemon water to prepare your body for the day.

Movement:

Standing in Mountain Position, interlace your fingers behind your back. Roll the shoulders to the back body and tilt the chin to the ceiling. Take three cleansing breaths over the front side of the heart. This allows the tension to roll off our shoulders while opening the heart and throat chakras.

Day 1 Evening

Nourishment:

Enjoying a cup of hot lemon water to help slow your body and mind down for restoration.

Slowing the movement:

From a comfortable reclined restorative position, place both hands on the belly. Recognize the rise and fall of the breath. Relax in silence for a minimum of 2 minutes.

Silence, stillness and centering on:
I am kindhearted, I am peaceful, I am loving.

Devotional:

Jude 1:2 – The Voice

Kindness, peace and love – may they never stop blooming in you and from you.

If you are good at visualization, you might try visualizing a vine rooted in your heart centre then having vines growing up to the crown and down to the souls of the feet. If we can cultivate that kindness, peace and love consistently in our body, mind and souls it will grow from us into our external lives. There, we are transforming ourselves and others.

Journal:

Review your day. How have you been able to create space in the body, mind and soul to allow love to blossom in and from you? What is holding you back or spurring you on? Journal those things you are thankful for and things you remain hopeful of.

Additional journal prompts for overall health and wellness:
~nourishment
~movement

Pray.

Day 2 Morning

Find a comfortable restorative pose, one hand on heart one hand on belly recognizing the breath as it flows through the body. Enjoy the silence and calmness for at least 2 minutes, paying attention to the breath, the gentle rise and fall of the chest and belly.

Silence, stillness and centering for a minimum of 2 minutes on:
I have faith, I have hope, I have love.

Devotional reading:

'Romans 13:8 The Voice

Don't owe anyone anything, with the exception of love to one another – that is a debt which never ends – because the person who loves others has fulfilled the law.'

When we share loving kindness and compassion with others we are fulfilling what God has asked us to do. Everything about God is about love. The Message bible uniquely states it in everyday terms: 'You can't go wrong when you love others. When you add up everything in the law code, the sum total is love'. So very true and if we stay captive to love, we are doing what we have been asked to do and love will not disappoint.

I have adapted the mentality that love never fails! I believe that love must be the motivation behind all that we do. I have incorporated some of my daily prayers from the teachings of Brother Paul as detailed in Peter Scazzero book *Emotionally Healthy Spirituality* perhaps my adapted prayers will stir your heart and help you love more:

Allow love to justify my actions. May I live love and let love invade me. Love will never fail to teach me what I should do. In the same way may God give me the courage to faithfully live my unique life in Christ and may love invade me. Love will never fail to teach me what I should do.

Often I will pray this prayer for other people:

(name or names) live love, let love invade you. It will never fail to teach you what you must do. In the same way (name or names) may God give you the courage to faithfully live your unique life in Christ. And may love invade you. It will never fail to teach you what you should do.

Love never hurts anyone and it achieves everything the law requires us to do.

Journal:

What came up for you while reading this devotion? Is it easy or hard to believe that love never fails? Pay attention to what stirs your heart today.

Morning Prayer:

Might I bravely love others today. Amen.

Nourishment:

Enjoy a cup of lemon water to prepare your body for the day.

Movement:

Standing in Mountain Position, interlace your fingers behind your back. Roll the shoulders to the back body and tilt the chin to the ceiling. Take three cleansing breaths over the front side of the heart. This allows the tension to roll off our shoulders while opening the heart and throat chakras.

Day 2 Evening

Nourishment:

Enjoying a cup of hot lemon water to help slow your body and mind down for restoration.

Slowing the movement:

From a comfortable reclined restorative position, place both hands on the belly. Recognize the rise and fall of the breath. Relax in silence for a minimum of 2 minutes.

Silence, stillness and centering on:
I am kindhearted, I am peaceful, I am loving.

Devotional:

First a small excerpt from 1 Thessalonians 4:9-12 The Message: Regarding life together and getting along with each other, you don't need me to tell you what to do. You're God taught in these matters. Just love one another! You're already good at it...Keep it up; get better and better at it.

1 Thessalonians 5:12-18 The Message

And now, friends, we ask you to honor those leaders who work so hard for you, who have been given the responsibility of urging and guiding you along your obedience. Overwhelm them with appreciation and love!

Get along among yourselves, each of you doing your part...Gently encourage the stragglers, and reach out for the exhausted, pulling them to their feet. Be patient with each person, attentive to individual needs. And be careful that when you get on each other's nerves you don't snap at each other. Look for the best in each other, and always do your best to bring it out.

Be cheerful no matter what; pray all the time; thank God no matter what happens. This is the way God wants you who belong to Christ Jesus to live.

And a small excerpt from 1 Thessalonians 4:9-12 The Passion says: God is continually teaching you to unselfishly love one another...let this unselfish love increase and flow through you more and more. Aspire to lead a calm and peaceful life as you mind your own business and earn your living...by doing this you will live an honorable life, influencing others and commanding respect of even the unbelievers. Then focusing on 1 Thessalonians 5:14-18: Be skilled at gently encouraging those who feel themselves inadequate. Be faithful to stand your ground. Help the weak to stand again. Be quick to demonstrate patience with everyone. Resist revenge, and make sure that no one pays back evil in place of evil but always pursue doing what is beautiful to one another and to all the unbelievers. Let joy be your continual feast. Make your life a prayer. And in the midst of everything be always giving thanks, for this is God's perfect plan for you in Christ Jesus.

I love comparing different translations to see what stirs my heart. These are two translations that say the same thing but in different ways. As you read through it slowly a few times ask the Holy Spirit to help you form a prayer for your daily walk in the wake of love. Three takeaways I will note are: 1.) Be thankful and remember others in your prayers who have been an encouragement in your healing journey 2.) Be thankful to God as he is continually teaching you to unselfishly love others and 3.) Be accepting and pursue doing what is beautiful to believers and unbelievers alike.

Journal:

Review your day. How have you been able to create space in the body, mind and soul to allow divine love to lift you up and allow you to demonstrate unselfish love to others? Where could you have leaned more into love? Journal those things you are thankful for and things you remain hopeful of.

Additional journal prompts for overall health and wellness:
~nourishment
~movement

Pray.

Day 3 Morning

Find a comfortable restorative pose, one hand on heart one hand on belly recognizing the breath as it flows through the body. Enjoy the silence and calmness for at least 2 minutes, paying attention to the breath, the gentle rise and fall of the chest and belly.

Silence, stillness and centering for a minimum of 2 minutes on:
I have faith, I have hope, I have love.

Devotional reading:

Hearts Refreshed

> Joy catches us off guard. It is a response that wells up in our hearts form love. We can't control it, and we can't bring it about. We don't find joy; it finds us, often surprising us when it arrives, making us smile for no apparent reason, break into a tune when no one is around to hear it, or trust peacefully when things are falling down around our ears. Joy is never tied to wealth or circumstances or conditions, only love. A person who has every material possession might never experience joy, while someone who has nothing the world considers valuable may have joy like a rushing river. If you know love, you'll be surprised by joy.

Nicole Johnson
Women of Faith Devotional Bible

This quote is a lovely reminder that when our hearts are refreshed it creates space to feel joy and allows love to bloom. I encourage you to invite the Holy Spirit to surprise you and spur you on to refresh your heart throughout this day and everyday.

Journal:

What came up for you while reading this devotion? Joy is a choice; how will you choose joy? What intentions are you setting for yourself today? Pay attention to what stirs your heart today.

Morning Prayer:

May my heart be refreshed by your Love and may I see great joy today. Amen.

Nourishment:

Enjoy a cup of lemon water to prepare your body for the day.

Movement:

Standing in Mountain Position, interlace your fingers behind your back. Roll the shoulders to the back body and tilt the chin to the ceiling. Take three cleansing breaths over the front side of the heart. This allows the tension to roll off our shoulders while opening the heart and throat chakras.

Day 3 Evening

Nourishment:

Enjoying a cup of hot lemon water to help slow your body and mind down for restoration.

Slowing the movement:

From a comfortable reclined restorative position, place both hands on the belly. Recognize the rise and fall of the breath. Relax in silence for a minimum of 2 minutes.

Silence, stillness and centering on:
I am kindhearted, I am peaceful, I am loving.

Devotional:

1 Corinthians 14:1 The Message

Go after a life of love as if your life depended on it – because it does.

Go ahead and read that scripture a few times. Let it sink in. I assert that our life and our wellbeing actually does depend on us going after a life of love. When we allow that love to bloom in the heart, then in and through us the healing transforms our innermost beings and the human beings closest to us.

Journal:

Reviewing your day, how have you been able to create space in the body, mind and soul to allow love to blossom in and from you? What is holding you back or spurring to live a life of love as if your life depended on it? Journal those things you are thankful for and things you remain hopeful of.

Additional journal prompts for overall health and wellness:
~nourishment
~movement

Pray.

Day 4 Morning

Find a comfortable restorative pose, one hand on heart one hand on belly recognizing the breath as it flows through the body. Enjoy the silence and calmness for at least 2 minutes, paying attention to the breath, the gentle rise and fall of the chest and belly.

Silence, stillness and centering for a minimum of 2 minutes on:
I have faith, I have hope, I have love.

Devotional reading:

There is an old country and western song, *Believe* by Brooks & Dunn, that talks about "the words written in red" those are the most important words because those are the words spoken by Jesus. His words never fail to give us meaning and direction for our lives. In John 15:12 (Amplified Bible) Jesus provides the following direction:

> This is My commandment, that you love and unselfishly seek the best for one another, just as I have loved you.

Jesus wants us to be an on-ramp to help others, to build others up and spread his love, joy and peace everywhere we step.

Sometimes showing love can be difficult, especially in annoying or frustrating situations. When we show acts of love in our everyday circumstances, love will start to bloom in and through us. It will also help bloom love in others. Finding little ways to lift others up is a good way to practice love blooming.

Journal:

What came up for you while reading this devotion? How might you find a little way of love to lift someone up today? Pay attention to what stirs your heart today.

Morning Prayer:

Grant me the wisdom to find ways to show love in all my circumstances. Give me pause to show love even as I encounter annoying and frustrating situations today. Amen.

Nourishment:

Enjoy a cup of lemon water to prepare your body for the day.

Movement:

Standing in Mountain Position, interlace your fingers behind your back. Roll the shoulders to the back body and tilt the chin to the ceiling. Take three cleansing breaths over the front side of the heart. This allows the tension to roll off our shoulders while opening the heart and throat chakras.

Day 4 Evening

Nourishment:

Enjoying a cup of hot lemon water to help slow your body and mind down for restoration.

Slowing the movement:

From a comfortable reclined restorative position, place both hands on the belly. Recognize the rise and fall of the breath. Relax in silence for a minimum of 2 minutes.

Silence, stillness and centering on:
I am kindhearted, I am peaceful, I am loving.

Devotional:

Nehemiah 8:10 The Voice

Do not grieve over your past mistakes. Let the Eternal's own joy be your protection!

Sometimes our minds can be our enemies and we ruminate over our past failings or mistakes. I find it helpful to set daily reminders in my agenda to remind me to forgive myself and others for past mistakes. Setting these reminders and receiving those notifications to my phone is like receiving a prayer from heaven that has allowed me to be thankful for lessons learned. Find joy and peace in forgiveness.

Journal:

Review your day. How have you been able to create space in the body, mind and soul to allow love to blossom in and from you? Was your heart refreshed today knowing The Eternal's own joy is your protection and strength? Journal those things you are thankful for and things you remain hopeful of.

Additional journal prompts for overall health and wellness:
~nourishment
~movement

Pray.

Day 5 Morning

Find a comfortable restorative pose, one hand on heart one hand on belly recognizing the breath as it flows through the body. Enjoy the silence and calmness for at least 2 minutes, paying attention to the breath, the gentle rise and fall of the chest and belly.

Silence, stillness and centering for a minimum of 2 minutes on:

I have faith, I have hope, I have love.

Devotional reading:

1 Corinthians 13:3-7 The Message

> Love never gives up.
> Love cares more for others than for self.
> Love doesn't want what it doesn't have.
> Love doesn't strut,
> Doesn't have a swelled head,
> Doesn't force itself on others,
> Isn't always "me first,"
> Doesn't fly off the handle,
> Doesn't keep score of the sins of others,
> Doesn't revel when others grovel,
> Takes pleasure in the flowering of truth,
> Puts up with anything,
> Trusts God always,
> Always looks for the best,
> Never looks back,
> But keeps going to the end.

This is a scripture that is good to come back to from time to time. I have a shortened up version that I pray daily. Over the years different phrases stood out for different reasons. For me and my ability to remain content in any and all circumstances I remember that love doesn't want what love doesn't have. Knowing this has helped me bring my wandering mind back to the calmness and comfort of my heart where I know I have Jesus in my heart and I can always rely on that. It allows me to align my vertical and anchor myself to the One that gives me strength. Being anchored to that kind of love, it is easier to have that trust in God and always look for the silver lining in any and all circumstances. We all have different circumstances and different phrases might stir your heart. At different stages of my own healing journey different phrases nudged my heart. I encourage you to invite the Holy Spirit with you as you read it slowly a few times.

Journal:

What came up for you while reading this devotion? Which of these phrases stirred your heart? What phrases landed heavy? Why?

Morning Prayer:

Grant me the wisdom to find ways to show love in all my circumstances. Give me pause to show love and improve my ability to love. Amen.

Nourishment:

Enjoy a cup of lemon water to prepare your body for the day.

Movement:

Standing in Mountain Position, interlace your fingers behind your back. Roll the shoulders to the back body and tilt the chin to the ceiling. Take three cleansing breaths over the front side of the heart. This allows the tension to roll off our shoulders while opening the heart and throat chakras.

Day 5 Evening

Nourishment:

Enjoying a cup of hot lemon water to help slow your body and mind down for restoration.

Slowing the movement:

From a comfortable reclined restorative position, place both hands on the belly. Recognize the rise and fall of the breath. Relax in silence for a minimum of 2 minutes.

Silence, stillness and centering on:
I am kindhearted, I am peaceful, I am loving.

Devotional:

Matthew 19:19 The Passion

…love those around you as you love yourself.

If you are able to visualize, think about the heart and visualize those vines of love growing in you then visualize them growing around those that are closest to you. Some people are better with colour visualisations, if so try using the colours pink or green (which are colours linked associated with the heart chakra) and send that flowing energy from yourself to those that are in your circle of love.

Journal:

Review your day. How have you been able to create space in the body, mind and soul to allow love to blossom in and from you? How did you show love to others today? Journal those things you are thankful for and things you remain hopeful of.

Additional journal prompts for overall health and wellness:
~nourishment
~movement

Pray.

Throughout this Segment - Love Blooming - we talked about the invitation to allow love to bloom. I believe that love is like a seed planted in the garden of our heart. If it is cultivated and nourished it will blossom. When we surrender our hearts to the One who first loved us we provide the nourishment that body, mind and soul requires to bloom. As we demonstrate lovingkindness within our horizontal reach we become that rain worm in His vineyard.

SEGMENT 3

~

Fruits of the Spirit

Through this segment we will take an in-depth look at the Fruits of the Spirit. This verse in the bible is very dear to my heart. I will provide ways in which you can meditate on this scripture, pray this scripture and allow this scripture to help you learn more about yourself and areas of your life or patterns in your life that you may need to recognize. I will also provide direction on how to refresh your patterns to make the necessary changes.

The methodology of this segment came to me in a peculiar way. Sometimes it takes us a while to understand how God or the Holy Spirit is speaking in our lives, and early in my journey, I was by no means catching all the cues. For nearly a week straight I was waking up at 5:22 am, even on days I did not need to be up that early. I finally realized there was a message in that and I began to think about 5:22 scriptures that might be relevant. I stopped hard on Galatians 5:22 where it speaks to the Fruits of the Spirit. After meditating on that scripture it became very clear that I needed to work on unconditional love. My heart was stirred and I allowed the Spirit to guide me to where I needed healing.

When we allow ourselves to receive, when we become willing participants to listen and learn we can engage the deep healing required to move to the next level of our journey.

I now pray that scripture daily, as a tune up. I find there is always something that we can improve. We are human and fall short of glory. This scripture helps keep me anchored.

Day 1 Morning

Find a comfortable restorative pose, one hand on heart one hand on belly recognizing the breath as it flows through the body. Enjoy the silence and calmness for at least 2 minutes, paying attention to the breath, the gentle rise and fall of the chest and belly.

Silence, stillness and centering for a minimum of 2 minutes on:
I am happy, I am healthy, I am free.

Devotional reading:

In Galatians 5, Paul preaches about freedom. This freedom comes from the atoning sacrifice of Jesus. We have been set free, not partially free, but completely and wonderfully free! As free people, the Spirit gives us characteristics of Jesus and allows us to freely love in joy and peace. We must always cherish this truth and stubbornly refuse to go back into the bondage of our past. (Galatians 5:1 The Passion) It is our choice to accept and live in this freedom taking on our Christ-like qualities. In this space of freedom, Jesus gives us patience along with kindness and faithfulness. We can reflect the goodness of God while being gentle to ourselves and others as we establish healthy boundaries in our lives and respect the healthy boundaries in the lives of others. It is important to have a gentle understanding that we are each on a unique journey, especially those of us who have chosen a Spirit filled wellness path. As we learn to navigate our walk with Christ we establish healthy ways to operate with self-control. For those who follow Him and live in the Spirit, these characteristics (or fruits) are a gift from God. As we grow in the faith, we find that we belong to God and can walk daily in the Spirit.

The Holy Spirit produces different kinds of fruit: unconditional love, joy, peace, patience, kindheartedness, goodness, faithfulness, gentleness and self-control. You won't find any law opposed to fruit like this. Those of us who belong to the Anointed One have crucified our old lives and put to death the flesh and all the lusts and desires that plague us. Now since we have chosen to walk with the Spirit, let's keep each step in perfect sync with God's Spirit. This will happen when we set aside our self-interests and work together to create true community, instead of a culture consumed by provocation, pride and envy.

(adapted from Galatians 5:22-26 The Voice)

As we allow ourselves to take on these Christ-like qualities it strengthens the core of who we are and securely anchors our vertical to the love of God. Whereby allowing our interactions and relationships we have on the horizontal to be patient, kind, gentle and demonstrating self-control.

Journal:

What came up for you while reading this devotion? What intentions are you setting for yourself today? What are you wanting to take forward and think about today?

Morning Prayer:

May I walk in the spirit today. May my fruits flourish in all circumstances. Amen.

Nourishment:

Enjoy a cup of lemon water to prepare your body for the day.

Movement:

Standing in Mountain Position, interlace your fingers behind your back. Roll the shoulders to the back body and tilt the chin to the ceiling. Take three cleansing breaths over the front side of the heart. This allows the tension to roll off our shoulders while opening the heart and throat chakras.

Day 1 Evening

Nourishment:

Enjoying a cup of hot lemon water to help slow your body and mind down for restoration.

Slowing the movement:

From a comfortable reclined restorative position, place both hands on the belly. Recognize the rise and fall of the breath. Relax in silence for a minimum of 2 minutes.

Silence, stillness and centering on:
I am peaceful, I am patient, I am loving.

Devotional:

Galatians 5:22-23 The Passion

> But fruit produced by the Holy Spirit within you is
> divine love in all its varied expressions:
>
> joy that overflows,
> peace that subdues,
> patience that endures,
> kindness in action,
> a life full of virtue,
> faith that prevails,
> gentleness of heart, and
> strength of spirit.
>
> Never set the law above these qualities, for they are
> meant to be limitless.

These Christ-like qualities are truly life giving, divine
love and a freedom we all need in our lives. Read slowly
through that scripture again while asking the Holy
Spirit to highlight what phrase is most meaningful in
your life today.

Journal:

Review your day. How have you been able to create space in the body, mind and soul to allow your fruits to grow? What is holding you back or spurring you on? Journal those things you are thankful for and things you remain hopeful of.

Additional journal prompts for overall health and wellness:
~nourishment
~movement

Pray.

Day 2 Morning

Find a comfortable restorative pose, one hand on heart one hand on belly recognizing the breath as it flows through the body. Enjoy the silence and calmness for at least 2 minutes, paying attention to the breath, the gentle rise and fall of the chest and belly.

Silence, stillness and centering for a minimum of 2 minutes on:
I am happy, I am healthy, I am free.

Devotional reading:

Today we will reflect on Peter Scazzero's discussion about God making our lives beautiful. This reading has enriched my spiritual journey and I thought it would be a good way to end off this week of focusing on the fruits of the Spirit.

"The apostle Paul recorded: "What happens when we live (authentically) God's way? He brings gifts into our lives, much the same way fruit appears in an orchard" (Galatians 5:22 MSG). Using two popular versions of the Bible, let me demonstrate how Paul described these beautiful fruits in Galatians 5:22-23:

NIV	The Message
Love	Affection for others
Joy	Exuberance about life
Peace	Serenity
Patience	A willingness to stick with things
Kindness	A sense of compassion in the heart
Goodness	A conviction that a basic holiness permeates things and people
Faithfulness	Involved in loyal commitments
Gentleness	Not needing to force our way in life

Self-Control   Able to marshal and direct our energies wisely

God promises if you and I will do life his way (even though it feels unnatural and hard to us initially) then our lives will be beautiful.

Take a few moments to pause in your reading. Read the previous list slowly and prayerfully, letting each word soak into you. Ask yourself honestly: "To what degree are these fruits realities in my life today?" Think about yourself at home, work, school, church. Allow God to love you where you are now. Ask him to do his work - in you, that you might become the kind of person described in the previous passage.

Journal:

What came up for you while reading this devotion? What fruit stirred something in your heart? What fruit will you intentionally focus on today?

Morning Prayer:

May I walk in the spirit today. May my fruits flourish in all circumstances. Amen.

Nourishment:

Enjoy a cup of lemon water to prepare your body for the day.

Movement:

Standing in Mountain Position, interlace your fingers behind your back. Roll the shoulders to the back body and tilt the chin to the ceiling. Taking three cleansing breaths over the front side of the heart. This allows the tension to roll off our shoulders while opening the heart and throat chakras.

Day 2 Evening

Nourishment:

Enjoying a cup of hot lemon water to help slow your body and mind down for restoration.

Slowing the movement:

From a comfortable reclined restorative position, place both hands on the belly. Recognize the rise and fall of the breath. Relax in silence for a minimum of 2 minutes.

Silence, stillness and centering on:
I am peaceful, I am patient, I am loving.

Devotional reading:

"Emotions accompany all the events of our lives. If you have a broken relationship, chances are you'll likely feel lonely. If you're unjustly accused, you'll probably feel angry. The more importance you assign to the event, the more intensely you'll feel the emotion…

What we hold in high esteem will eventually govern us, but what we hold in low esteem, we will govern. Yes, we need to acknowledge our feelings, but we should never regard them more highly than God's Word. Don't ever bow to your feelings because you hold them in such high regard. Instead, make them bow to your God."

-Jennifer Rothschild
Lessons I Learned in the Dark

Managing the line between diving into emotion and letting the emotions govern our lives takes self-control, perseverance and patience. By having a healthy (self-controlled) response to our emotions (the events or circumstances on our horizontal) we create a space (pause) to introduce those things we struggle with to our God. Whatever is causing waves, friction or disturbances bring it back to the vertical, to the Christ-like qualities within you.

Journal:

Review your day. How have you been able to create space in the body, mind and soul to allow your fruits to grow? Are there ways you can think of that will allow you to let your feelings bow to God? What is holding you back or spurring you on? Journal those things you are thankful for and things you remain hopeful of.

Additional journal prompts for overall health and wellness:
~nourishment
~movement

Pray.

Day 3 Morning

Find a comfortable restorative pose, one hand on heart one hand on belly recognizing the breath as it flows through the body. Enjoy the silence and calmness for at least 2 minutes, paying attention to the breath, the gentle rise and fall of the chest and belly.

Silence, stillness and centering for a minimum of 2 minutes on:

I am happy, I am healthy, I am free.

Devotional reading:

The Amplified version of the bible discusses that the Fruit of the Spirit is a result of His presence within us.

Love (unselfish concern for others),
Joy,
(inner) Peace,
Patience (not the ability to wait, but how we act while waiting),
Kindness,
Goodness,
Faithfulness,
Gentleness,
Self-control.

(adapted from the Amplified Bible)

I did a full stop at Patience (not the ability to wait, but how we act while waiting). Patience for ourselves, for others and for God can be difficult. Allowing the Spirit to work in and through us receptively will provide us grace as we wait.

Journal:

What came up for you while reading this devotion? What stirred your heart today? How can you navigate your day showing unselfish love for others? What needs to happen to maintain that inner peace? How will you act while being patient?

Morning Prayer:

May I walk in the spirit today. May my fruits flourish in all circumstances. Amen.

Nourishment:

Enjoy a cup of lemon water to prepare your body for the day.

Movement:

Standing in Mountain Position, interlace your fingers behind your back. Roll the shoulders to the back body and tilt the chin to the ceiling. Take three cleansing breaths over the front side of the heart. This allows the tension to roll off our shoulders while opening the heart and throat chakras.

Day 3 Evening

Nourishment:

Enjoying a cup of hot lemon water to help slow your body and mind down for restoration.

Slowing the movement:

From a comfortable reclined restorative position, place both hands on the belly. Recognize the rise and fall of the breath. Relax in silence for a minimum of 2 minutes.

Silence, stillness and centering on:
I am peaceful, I am patient, I am loving.

Devotional:

> Friendship is the fruit gathered from the trees planted in rich soil of love, and nurtured with tender care and understanding.

> - Alma L. Weixelbaum

Take a moment to send gratitude and reflect upon those fruit trees planted in the rich soil of the divine love that resides in you. Remembering the meaning behind Proverbs 17:17 ...a friend loves at all times.

Journal:

Review your day. How have you been able to create space in the body, mind and soul to allow your fruits to grow? What seeds of kindness did you plant today? Journal those things you are thankful for and things you remain hopeful of.

Additional journal prompts for overall health and wellness:
~nourishment
~movement

Pray.

Day 4 Morning

Find a comfortable restorative pose, one hand on heart one hand on belly recognizing the breath as it flows through the body. Enjoy the silence and calmness for at least 2 minutes, paying attention to the breath, the gentle rise and fall of the chest and belly.

Silence, stillness and centering for a minimum of 2 minutes on:
I am happy, I am healthy, I am free.

Devotional reading:

2 Timothy 1:7 The Message

God doesn't want us to be shy with his gifts, but bold and loving and sensible.

"Faith in God gives your life a center from which you can reach out and dare to love the world."

- Barbara Farmer

Loving the world means sharing our gifts, our fruits of the Spirit. As we listen to the direction of the Spirit we become more and more obedient to His calling on our lives. It is through our experience, our own testimonies, that we can allow our servant heart to help others. It might be scary at first but each step you take outside your comfort zone you step further into your faith and your purpose.

Journal:

What came up for you while reading this devotion? What intentions are you setting for yourself today to be less shy about your gifts? Where can you reach out of your comfort zone and love the world today.

Morning Prayer:

May I be comfortable spreading loving kindness everywhere I step today. Amen.

Nourishment:

Enjoy a cup of lemon water to prepare your body for the day.

Movement:

Standing in Mountain Position, interlace your fingers behind your back. Roll the shoulders to the back body and tilt the chin to the ceiling. Taking three cleansing breaths over the front side of the heart. This allows the tension to roll off our shoulders while opening the heart and throat chakras.

Day 4 Evening

Nourishment:

Enjoying a cup of hot lemon water to help slow your body and mind down for restoration.

Slowing the movement:

From a comfortable reclined restorative position, place both hands on the belly. Recognize the rise and

fall of the breath. Relax in silence for a minimum of 2 minutes.

Silence, stillness and centering on:
I am peaceful, I am patient, I am loving.

Devotional:

John 15:2 NIV

Every branch that does bear fruit he prunes so that it will be even more fruitful.

Be open to the pruning in your life. All growing things bloom more beautifully after they're pruned.

- Joy Wisehart

Take a moment to reflect the pruning that has happened in your life. Where can you be more open to pruning?

Journal:

Review your day. How have you been able to create space in the body, mind and soul to allow pruning for future growth? What is holding you back or spurring you on? Journal those things you are thankful for and things you remain hopeful of.

Additional journal prompts for overall health and wellness:
~nourishment
~movement

Pray.

Day 5 Morning

Find a comfortable restorative pose, one hand on heart one hand on belly recognizing the breath as it flows through the body. Enjoy the silence and calmness for at least 2 minutes, paying attention to the breath, the gentle rise and fall of the chest and belly.

Silence, stillness and centering for a minimum of 2 minutes on:
I am happy, I am healthy, I am loving.

Devotional reading:

> Dare to love and to be a real friend. The love you give and receive is a reality that will lead you closer and closer to God as well as to those whom God has given you to love.

> - Henri J.M. Nouwen

It is true God puts people and situations in our lives so that we can grow our fruits of the Spirit. Sometimes this isn't easy. However, those are growth opportunities not annoyances. Sometimes it is self-control and patience that needs to be pruned so that we can grow ourselves or help others find growth on their journey. God has a purpose for everything, the good and the bad, every season and circumstance we face.

Journal:

What came up for you while reading this devotion? What intentions are you setting to love daringly today?

Morning Prayer:

Today I will dare to love all people in my life. Amen.

Nourishment:

Enjoy a cup of lemon water to prepare your body for the day.

Movement:

Standing in Mountain Position, interlace your fingers behind your back. Roll the shoulders to the back body and tilt the chin to the ceiling. Taking three cleansing breaths over the front side of the heart. This allows the tension to roll off our shoulders while opening the heart and throat chakras.

Day 5 Evening

Nourishment:

Enjoying a cup of hot lemon water to help slow your body and mind down for restoration.

Slowing the movement:

From a comfortable reclined restorative position, place both hands on the belly. Recognize the rise and fall of the breath. Relax in silence for a minimum of 2 minutes.

Silence, stillness and centering on:
I am peaceful, I am patient, I am loving.

Devotional:

John 15:4 The Voice

Abide in Me, and I will abide in you. A branch cannot bear fruit if it is disconnected from the vine, and neither will you if you are not connected to Me.

When we abide in Jesus, our walk begins to take on Christ-like characteristics. Our walk becomes more fluid and graceful as we create space for the indwelling of the Holy Spirit. As we let the Spirit dwell within us, our outward characteristics start to change our relationships with everything on our journey and within our lives. As we work on the fruits of the Spirit we are allowing our God to shape us and reshape us as we grow in our faith and our spirituality.

Journal:

Do a personal inventory of areas of self improvement on your week. Is it easy or hard to invite the indwelling of the Holy Spirit? Has it been easy or hard to bring things captive to the heart space? Journal those things you are thankful for and things you remain hopeful of.

Additional journal prompts for overall health and wellness:
~nourishment
~movement

Pray.

Throughout this segment - we took an indepth look at the fruits of the spirits. These fruits are a gift from Jesus so that we can be better versions of ourselves in our day to day lives. This starts by acknowledging the indwelling of the Holy Spirit and accepting the unconditional love of He who made the atoning sacrifice for all sinners. I have found that when I can walk in the wake of His love and demonstrate His characteristics my vertical is secure and there is so much more joy and peace on my horizontal.

I have found that understanding myself and unrooting my own motives (honest and healthy personal inventory) to gently approach my true self with a loving gaze has helped me love myself more and grow my Fruits of the Spirit.

SEGMENT 4

~

Going Back to Go Forward

On my personal journey there were some fundamental things I went *back* to, so that I could continue my way forward. I was unhealthy and stuck in unhealthy patterns. I went back to the basics in my spiritual life. I went back to simple and easy exercises and diet. I took an honest personal inventory (willingly or unwillingly) to establish a baseline. For me the serenity prayer was a helpful tool while doing my personal inventory:

> God grant me the serenity the accept the things I
> cannot change,
> Courage to change the things that I can;
> And wisdom to know the difference.

I went back to the simple prayer Jesus taught us to pray:

> Our Father,
> who art in heaven
> Hallowed be thy name
> Thy Kingdom come
> Thy will be done

On earth as it is in heaven.
Give us this day
Our daily bread
And forgive us our trespasses
As we forgive those who trespass against us.
And lead us not into temptation
But deliver us from evil
For thine is the Kingdom
The power and the glory.
Forever and ever. Amen

I also recited Psalm 51:10-12

Create in me a clean heart, O God,
and renew a right spirit within me.

Cast me not away from your presence, and take not
thy holy spirit from me.

Restore unto me the joy of your salvation, and
uphold me with a willing spirit.

I made small adjustments to my diet. Eating to the National Food Guide and using an elimination diet to give my body a rest from the things that were holding me back from healing. I began drinking more water and substituting water for the less healthy drinks I was consuming.

Following a hospital visit and being placed on a surgery wait list, I was sent to physical therapy for my back pain. It was at this time that I recognized the stretches the therapist suggested were, in fact, yoga poses. At that stage of my life I had done yoga, but I hadn't yet embraced it as a lifestyle. In addition to the physical therapy I also reconnected with a dear family friend that teaches Bikram yoga and, with her guidance, I started to set monthly goals. Goals of being able to get into certain poses as well as goals of being able to stay in a pose for a dedicated amount of time. Slowly, surely and prayerfully I got back to an exercise routine that worked on building my core strength.

Not only did I bring my newfound prayer life into my exercise routine, I started to bring my prayers into all the healthy improvements I was making in my life. What I found was, as my prayer life met my other activities, I began to see progress in leaps and bounds. Not to mention, the joy these activities were bringing to my body, mind and soul.

Segment 4 will focus on stepping back to enrich your forward momentum. In doing so, we will be dealing with things in the past which will help us recognize, realign and move forward. By bringing prayer into our personal inventories we can effectively forgive, let go and move on.

Segment 4 is also the movement past day 21 where you should start to see positive changes in your life, which gives you the momentum to keep on keeping on!

Day 1 Morning

Find a comfortable restorative pose, one hand on heart one hand on belly recognizing the breath as it flows through the body. Enjoy the silence and calmness for at least 2 minutes, paying attention to the breath, the gentle rise and fall of the chest and belly.

Silence, stillness and centering for a minimum of 2 minutes on:
I am peaceful. I am safe. I am free.

Devotional reading:

Ephesians 5:1-2 The Message

> Mostly what God does is love you. Keep company with him and learn a life of love. Observe how Christ loved us. His love was not cautious but extravagant. He didn't love in order to get something from us but to give everything of himself to us. Love like that.

When we take apart the extravagant love that God demonstrates for us it includes his offer to freely forgive us all our sins. The biggest gift we can give others is our ability to forgive. Now, forgiving is not forgetting or shifting blame or saying what happened was okay. The act of forgiving frees ourselves and others. It is simply not letting the infraction that cut into you have room in your heart. Peace can be obtained through praying for those who have wounded us. Nailing it to the cross, so to speak, and letting it go. When your mind wanders back to thoughts of the hurt or wound, remember that it is coming up to come out. Receive it, acknowledge it, pray for it and let it go.

In the same way, we too have done our own hurt on ourselves and others. We need to be able to offer that same forgiveness to ourselves. Forgiveness is an 'F' word most people do not want to deal with, but there is much healing in the release of an infraction and allowing forgiveness to fill its space.

The past will visit us at every level of our healing. I look at it as an opportunity to grow and send up gratitude and love for the experience that has built the person I am today!

Journal:

What came up for you while reading this devotion? Where can you show extravagant love today? Where can you open up to forgiveness?

Morning Prayer:

Help me find peace through forgiveness. Amen.

Nourishment:

Enjoy a cup of lemon water to prepare your body for the day.

Movement:

Standing in Mountain Position, interlace your fingers behind your back. Roll the shoulders to the back body and tilt the chin to the ceiling. Take three cleansing breaths over the front side of the heart. This allows the tension to roll off our shoulders while opening the heart and throat chakras.

Day 1 Evening

Nourishment:

Enjoying a cup of hot lemon water to help slow your body and mind down for restoration.

Slowing the movement:

From a comfortable reclined restorative position, place both hands on the belly. Recognize the rise and

fall of the breath. Relax in silence for a minimum of 2 minutes.

Silence, stillness and centering on:
I am grateful, I am forgiving, I am at peace.

Devotional:

Philippians 1:9 NLT

I pray that your love will overflow more and more, and that you will keep on growing in knowledge and understanding.

Journal:

Review your day. How have you been able to create space in the body, mind and soul to be overflowing in love today? What is holding you back or spurring you on? Was forgiveness hard or easy today? Journal those things you are thankful for and things you remain hopeful of.

Additional journal prompts for overall health and wellness:
~nourishment
~movement

Pray.

Day 2 Morning

Find a comfortable restorative pose, one hand on heart one hand on belly recognizing the breath as it flows through the body. Enjoy the silence and calmness for at least 2 minutes, paying attention to the breath, the gentle rise and fall of the chest and belly.

Silence, stillness and centering for a minimum of 2 minutes on:
I am peaceful. I am safe. I am free.

Devotional reading:

Through my Lenten journey a couple years ago, I came across this wonderful reading from Phyllis Zagano's *Loving Others* that really helped me with forgiveness.

> There is nothing more destructive than carrying a grudge throughout life. It is like a sack of rocks that only gets heavier, mainly because we keep adding to it. Yet, we insist on carrying all those rocks around. We even insist on picking up a few pebbles or stones from our memories along the way, adding to the burden of anger that weighs us down.
>
> I have been that way. Like the rest of humanity, I have been wronged, sometimes by people I trusted and respected. I am not talking about being cut off

on the highway by a stranger, or suffering a smart remark from a colleague in the parking lot. Like you, there are positions I thought I should have gotten, into which I put an extraordinary amount of time and effort, all of which came to naught.

But did it? Did my seeking what I eventually could not have really cause that much difficulty in my life? Or did I cause my own difficulty by not letting go of the experience and by not accepting the results?

If I place the cast of characters in my mind for any of the many times I have been wronged, or have been treated unfairly, I would literally need more room! Then what happens? I simply have no room in my mind for anything else. The events or incidents plays and replays like the repetitive call of the cuckoo bird, not stopping and certainly not giving me any peace. If I hang on to these old memories, and replay them like old movies in my mind, I will create in myself the same feelings I had when I was first wronged. To be sure, there are instances in my life and in your when we have been genuinely wronged. But to replay the scenario over and over does nothing but dig the hurt deeper and deeper into the psyche.

I am not suggesting to forget about everything. I am suggesting…that one way to lessen the pain is to pray for those who have hurt you. That does not mean bringing them to mind every minute of the day. What it does mean is to place them in God's care when they do appear in your thought, even if it happens to be every minute of the day.

...We do not need to excuse wrongs, or even to forget them, but we must always forgive.

What Phyllis is saying here is we all have the same internal opportunities for a life of peace and happiness. "By way of analogy, we are taught that we all have the same sun shining on us and we all have the same rain falling on us. It is how we deal with sun and rain, how we deal with the happy and the not-so-happy things of life that causes our interior weather."

Journal:

What came up for you while reading this devotion? How will you deal with the interior weather throughout this day? What can you take forward and think about today?

Morning Prayer:

Grant me grace as I learn to forgive in the most difficult of situations. Amen.

Nourishment:

Enjoy a cup of lemon water to prepare your body for the day.

Movement:

Standing in Mountain Position, interlace your fingers behind your back. Roll the shoulders to the back body and tilt the chin to the ceiling. Take three cleansing breaths over the front side of the heart. This allows the tension to roll off our shoulders while opening the heart and throat chakras.

Day 2 Evening

Nourishment:

Enjoying a cup of hot lemon water to help slow your body and mind down for restoration.

Slowing the movement:

From a comfortable reclined restorative position, place both hands on the belly. Recognize the rise and fall of the breath. Relax in silence for a minimum of 2 minutes.

Silence, stillness and centering on:
I am grateful, I am forgiving, I am at peace.

Devotional:

Calm me. O Lord, as You stilled the storm.

Still me, O Lord, keep me from harm.
Let all the tumult within me cease,
Enfold me, Lord in your peace.

- Celtic Traditional

Journal:

Review your day. How have you been able to create space in the body, mind and soul to deal with the interior weather? Where were you able to calm the storm and find His peace? Journal those things you are thankful for and things you remain hopeful of.

Additional journal prompts for overall health and wellness:
~nourishment
~movement

Pray.

Day 3 Morning

Find a comfortable restorative pose, one hand on heart one hand on belly recognizing the breath as it flows through the body. Enjoy the silence and calmness for at least 2 minutes, paying attention to the breath, the gentle rise and fall of the chest and belly.

Silence, stillness and centering for a minimum of 2 minutes on:
I am peaceful. I am safe. I am free.

Devotional reading:

Colossians 3:12-15 The Voice

Since you are all set apart by God, made holy and dearly loved, clothe yourselves with a holy way of life: compassion, kindness, humility, gentleness and patience. Put up with one another. Forgive. Pardon any offenses against one another, as the Lord has pardoned you, because you should act in kind. But above all these, put on love! Love is the perfect tie to bind these together. Let your hearts fall under the rule of the Anointed's peace (the peace you were called to as one body), and be thankful.

I love this version of Colossians 3:12-15. It states: Forgive. Very clear, very plain. Forgive, period! Yet forgiveness of ourselves and others is difficult. The joy we feel afterwards is so uplifting, but many of us don't recognize how freeing and peaceful forgiveness can be. What makes it easier for me is to stay focused on love. Above all else, put on love. The vibration frequency of love is uplifting. When we focus on what matters to God, we allow the Holy Spirit to cultivate a gracious loving heart.

Journal:

What came up for you while reading this devotion? Where can you "put on love"? Which word stands out to you most: compassion, kindness, humility, gentleness and patience? How can you walk the holy way today?

Morning Prayer:

Help me find peace through forgiveness. Amen.

Nourishment:

Enjoy a cup of lemon water to prepare your body for the day.

Movement:

Standing in Mountain Position, interlace your fingers behind your back. Roll the shoulders to the back body

and tilt the chin to the ceiling. Take three cleansing breaths over the front side of the heart. This allows the tension to roll off our shoulders while opening the heart and throat chakras.

Day 3 Evening

Nourishment:

Enjoying a cup of hot lemon water to help slow your body and mind down for restoration.

Slowing the movement:

From a comfortable reclined restorative position, place both hands on the belly. Recognize the rise and fall of the breath. Relax in silence for a minimum of 2 minutes.

Silence, stillness and centering on:
I am grateful, I am forgiving, I am at peace.

Devotional:

1 Peter 4:8 The Voice

Most of all, love each other steadily and unselfishly because love makes up for many faults.

True fact, love covers a multitude of sins.

Journal:

Review your day. How have you been able to create space in the body, mind and soul to walk in a holy way today? What is holding you back or spurring you on? Was forgiveness hard or easy today? Journal those things you are thankful for and things you remain hopeful of.

Additional journal prompts for overall health and wellness:
~nourishment
~movement

Pray.

Day 4 Morning

Find a comfortable restorative pose, one hand on heart one hand on belly recognizing the breath as it flows through the body. Enjoy the silence and calmness for at least 2 minutes, paying attention to the breath, the gentle rise and fall of the chest and belly.

Silence, stillness and centering for a minimum of 2 minutes on:

I am peaceful. I am safe. I am free.

Devotional reading:

Colossians 3:12-15 NLT

Since God chose you to be the holy people he loves, you must clothe yourselves with tenderhearted mercy, kindness, humility, gentleness, and patience. Make allowances for each other's faults, and forgive anyone who offends you. Remember, the Lord forgave you, so you must forgive others. Above all, clothe yourselves with love, which binds us all together in perfect harmony. And let the peace that comes from Christ rule in your hearts. For as members of one body you are called to live in peace. And always be thankful.

This version of Colossians 3:12-15 is an important reminder that we need to "make allowances for each other's faults". We are each on a journey. We are each at different spots on our unique journey. It helps me be more patient when I activate my tenderhearted mercy, kindness and humility towards others. We all fall short of the glory of God. He is full of mercy for us; we should be as merciful towards others.

Journal:

What came up for you while reading this devotion? Where can you make allowances today for yourself and others? How will you clothe yourself today?

Morning Prayer:

Help me find peace through forgiveness. Amen.

Nourishment:

Enjoy a cup of lemon water to prepare your body for the day.

Movement:

Standing in Mountain Position, interlace your fingers behind your back. Roll the shoulders to the back body and tilt the chin to the ceiling. Take three cleansing breaths over the front side of the heart. This allows the tension to roll off our shoulders while opening the heart and throat chakras.

Day 4 Evening

Nourishment:

Enjoying a cup of hot lemon water to help slow your body and mind down for restoration.

Slowing the movement:

From a comfortable reclined restorative position, place both hands on the belly. Recognize the rise and

fall of the breath. Relax in silence for a minimum of 2 minutes.

Silence, stillness and centering on:
I am grateful, I am forgiving, I am at peace.

Devotional:

Making peace and moving on was something I struggled with until I practiced Lenting for the first time. During this first Lent journey I used the devotional *Sacred Silence* by Phillis Zagano. She discusses the difficulties we all have with anger, resentment and forgiveness and how making peace and moving is so important. Through my healing experience I have learned to make peace where I can. Sometimes it is not safe for ourselves or others to directly and personally make that peace. But as we make that peace we must add forgiveness from the stillness of our hearts. Remembering that forgiving is not forgetting, it is just the process of allowing the heart space to cultivate the matter to the point that you can pray for those who have hurt you or for the hurt you caused yourself or others. To me the forgiveness from the stillness of our hearts is like the magical pixie dust that flows over me that allows me to cultivate a grateful heart which gives me that freedom to make peace and move on. Making peace and moving on has provided me boldness and courage to pray for those who have deeply wounded me.

Forgiveness creates peace and peace allows us to keep moving on our journey. When we participate in the healing that forgiveness offers us it allows us to purge and free ourselves from matters in our life or circumstances from our past that bind us (try and keep us in the dark).

Forgiveness and letting go can be a difficult bumpy and sometimes curvy road. When we forgive and place those memories or circumstances at the foot of the cross we invite God's freedom to smooth our path so we can keep on keeping on!

Journal:

What came up for you while reading this devotion? Taking a personal inventory of your past, where can you forgive, let go and keep moving on into the freedom that comes from peace? How will you carry yourself today knowing this peace can be yours?

Additional journal prompts for overall health and wellness:
~nourishment
~movement

Pray.

Day 5 Morning

Find a comfortable restorative pose, one hand on heart one hand on belly recognizing the breath as it flows through the body. Enjoy the silence and calmness for at least 2 minutes, paying attention to the breath, the gentle rise and fall of the chest and belly.

Silence, stillness and centering for a minimum of 2 minutes on:
I am peaceful. I am safe. I am free.

Devotional reading:

In order to fulfill God's purpose in our lives, we need to be able to do everything without grumbling and arguing. We need to apply the mindset of Jesus within all our relationships. If we hold fast to His Word, the Word for our lives, then we can 'shine like stars in the sky'. Philippians 2 encourages us to imitate Christ's humility. Saint Paul speaks to the Philippians:

Philippians 2:1-4 The Voice

If you find any comfort from being in the Anointed, if His love brings you some encouragement, if you experience true companionship with the Spirit, if His tenderness and mercy fill your heart; then, brothers and sisters, here is one thing that would complete my joy - come together as one in mind and spirit and purpose, sharing in the same love. Don't let selfishness and prideful agendas take over. Embrace true humility, and lift your heads to extend love to others. Get beyond yourselves and protecting your own interests; be sincere, and secure your neighbors' interests first.

Journal:

What came up for you while reading this devotion? Where are selfishness and prideful agendas taking over your life? Where in your life today can you embrace true humility and lift your head to extend love to others?

Morning Prayer:

Help me find peace through forgiveness. Amen.

Nourishment:

Enjoy a cup of lemon water to prepare your body for the day.

Movement:

Standing in Mountain Position, interlace your fingers behind your back. Roll the shoulders to the back body

and tilt the chin to the ceiling. Take three cleansing breaths over the front side of the heart. This allows the tension to roll off our shoulders while opening the heart and throat chakras.

Day 5 Evening

Nourishment:

Enjoying a cup of hot lemon water to help slow your body and mind down for restoration.

Slowing the movement:

From a comfortable reclined restorative position, place both hands on the belly. Recognize the rise and fall of the breath. Relax in silence for a minimum of 2 minutes.

Silence, stillness and centering on:
I am grateful, I am forgiving, I am at peace.

Devotional:

Philippians 4:8 The Voice

Finally, brothers and sisters, fill your minds with beauty and truth. Meditate on whatever is right, whatever is pure, whatever is lovely, whatever is good, whatever is virtuous and praiseworthy.

Keeping to the type of script which Paul urges upon the Philippians will help us stay focused on the present moment. As we stay in the current moment our body, mind and soul will find true peace. God's peace!

Journal:

Review your day. How have you been able to create space in the body, mind and soul to be overflowing in love and humility today? What is holding you back or spurring you on? Where was your peace found today? Journal those things you are thankful for and things you remain hopeful of.

Additional journal prompts for overall health and wellness:
~nourishment
~movement

Pray.

In this segment we focused on the steps we need to take backward in order to gain forward momentum. When this happens you are not losing ground but gaining strength, stability and endurance. My experience has been that by this point in a 40 day program, I wanted to go deeper into my own healing. I wanted to dig deeper and build more spiritual strength. I have included some extra devotionals below that helped me at this stage of my journey:

Galatians 2:20 The Passion

My old identity has been co-crucified with Messiah and no longer lives; for the nails of his cross crucified me with him. And now the essence of this new life is no longer mine, for the Anointed One lives his life through me – we live in union as one! My new life is empowered by the faith of the Son of God who loves me so much that he gave himself for me, and dispenses his life into mine!

My visual for this when thoughts enter my mind that should not, is physically picking up a hammer and nailing that thought to the cross. Things come up so that they can come out which, allows God's peace to enter in.

Additional journal prompts:

How have you been able to create space in the body, mind and soul to be overflowing in peace and move on today? Is there a circumstance from your past that still has a grip on you? Are you able to nail it to the cross today? Journal what came up and out.

Ephesians 4:21-32 The Voice

If you have heard Jesus and have been taught by Him according to the truth that is in Him, then you know to take off your former way of life, your crumpled old self – that dark blot of a soul corrupted by deceitful desire and lust – take a fresh breath and to let God renew your attitude and spirit. Then you are ready to put on your new self, modeled after the very likeness of God: truthful, righteous, and holy.

So put away your lies and speak the truth to one another because we are all part of one another. When you are angry, don't let it carry you into sin. Don't let the sun set with anger in your heart or give the devil room to work...It's time to stop bringing grief to God's Holy Spirit; you have been sealed with the Spirit, marked as His own for the day of rescue. Banish bitterness, rage and anger, shouting and slander, and any and all malicious thoughts – these are poison. Instead, be kind and compassionate. Graciously forgive one another just as God has forgiven you through the Anointed, our Liberating King.

Additional journal prompts:

Do a personal inventory of areas of self improvement on your week. Is it easy or hard to invite the peace forgiveness brings? Walking like Jesus, is it easy or hard? Journal what came up when you read this scripture.

Ancient Meditation

The following ancient meditation is helpful for the process of going back to go forward. The concept of forgiveness is difficult for most people. The circumstances we face (or have faced) in our lives can cause us to hold onto matters that keep us bound to past hurt and pain. This wonderful meditation is a great centering prayer that can help cultivate the pixie dust of forgiveness found within the stillness of our hearts.

From a comfortable restorative position, take time to reflect on the Compassion Meditation Prayer found below. It originated from a Trappist Monk and I have come across this famous prayer in many books I have read. This prayer gets referenced in many wellness practices both from a Christian and secular perspective.

I have found it to be a helpful guide to pray over others when difficult situations or relationship differences arise. The purpose of this prayer is to help us forgive and let go of bitterness or conflict. Peter Scazzero details it in his book, Emotionally Healthy Relationships – Day by Day.

> May you be happy, may you be free.
> May you be loving, may you be loved.
> May you know the fulfillment of what God has planned for you.
> May you experience God's deep, profound love for you.
> May Jesus Christ be formed in you.
> May you know his peace that passes all understanding.
> May all good things be yours.
> May Jesus' joy be in you and may that joy be complete.
> May you know the Lord in all his goodness and compassion.
> May you be protected from the evil one amidst every temptation that comes your way.

May the Holy Spirit fill and permeate your entire
  being.
May you see his glory
May you be forgiven of every sin.
I forgive you (or "will try to forgive you") of every
  wound and hurt with all my heart.
May God's goodness and mercy follow you all the
  days of your life.

This ancient meditation assures us that it is no small task to pray for someone who has wounded us. However, as Scazzero goes on to say: "it is a significant step forward". I assert it is a brave step towards the narrow path or a brave surrender to stay on the narrow path. As I took the invitation from Scazzero and the others who placed this meditation in my path, allow me to extend the invite to you. I invite you to pray it repeatedly, even if you don't feel it. Know that having this meditation in your heart is pleasing to God and that healing blessings will be abundant. Trusting God will heal your wounds over time. Allow the Holy Spirit to do the work in and through you which you cannot do on your own. You will find the repetitiveness and the vibration of this meditation will soothe your body, mind and soul. I would also encourage you to tag this page so that you have it handy when you need it.

SEGMENT 5

~

Holy Listening

Where do you hear God speaking to you? To listen to God's voice we need to quiet the inner and outer noise so our hearts can open up and invite His word in. His word may come from the voice of a friend, a song that touches your heart, something you see or hear in nature and (of course) a scripture that might keep coming up in one way or another. Learning to be comfortable in the discomfort of quietness provides us the training and stamina to participate in holy listening.

As we learn to engage our holy listening skills we more enthusiastically invite the Holy Spirit to guide us and lead us down the narrow path. Our listening skills are like a road map for our lives.

I have learned to utilize 40 day prayer circles, worship music, labyrinth prayers, walking prayers, camino divina and lectio divina which have offered fascinating experiences with the Holy Spirit and sharpened my holy listening skills.

A 40 day prayer circle is something you can do alone or with a group. This is an ancient practice and has biblical significance. You can physically pray circles around what you are praying for, or you can journal and pray your prayer for 40 days. Remembering that prayer is a combination of us speaking to God and God speaking to us.

Worship music is just that. Music that inspires worship. It might be instrumental, it might be an old hymn, it might be a country and western song, whatever it is it stirs your heart and creates a space for you to worship God.

Labyrinth prayers are a relatively new prayer style for me. You walk intentionally and prayerfully into the labyrinth and prayerfully out while listening and allowing the Holy Spirit to guide you.

Camino divina is walking mindfully and intentionally as you pray. Similar to a labyrinth, I like to have a defined path for this walk. I offer camino divina events where I take clients or students to a top of a hill, we descend down prayerfully and intentionally on the ascent we listen. This practise is essentially praying, walking and listening.

Lectio divina is the act of meditating on a scripture for a set period of time. Reciting the scripture several times, leaving time between reading for holy listening.

Through the alignment of our chakras (energy in the body) we can utilize the body to help us with our holy listening. From my own experience with the energy system in our bodies — which I keep very attached to my Christian belief and spirituality — I have learned how to manage blocked energy which can aid *dis-ease* in the body. My goal is to help others understand the energy system of the body so that they can understand the energy in the body from a Christian perspective. The energy exists no matter our spiritual beliefs. If we as Christians can embrace the knowledge as God-given, we can find a healthy way to clear blocked energy in the body. There is not much information available yet on the kundalini effect from a Christian perspective. The phenomenon of kundalini energy is fascinating and, when harnessed, can help us better reach a point of spiritual connection with the creator of all things.

We have so much to learn about our bodies, mind and souls and the best place to start is engaging in silence so that the holy listening can occur!

Anything I have encountered on my journey, I have slowly and carefully checked against scriptures and with God to ensure that I am His good and faithful servant and I only want what is His pure, peaceful and sincere knowledge for my life.

Day 1 Morning

Find a comfortable restorative pose, one hand on heart one hand on belly recognizing the breath as it flows through the body. Enjoy the silence and calmness for at least 2 minutes, paying attention to the breath, the gentle rise and fall of the chest and belly.

Silence, stillness and centering for a minimum of 2 minutes on:
I am calm. I am peaceful. I am attentive.

Devotional reading:

Holy listening is an art in itself. I have studied this concept through my Holy Yoga masters training and through the teachings of Adele Ahberg Calhoun author of *Spiritual Disciplines Handbook – Practices That Transform Us*. Her handbook is an excellent tool for going deeper into a spiritual discipline journey. I continue to dig deeper on this topic and enjoy fascinating techniques of early Christian Mystics.

What I have found is our part in holy listening is to faithfully show up. Accept the invitation, ask the Holy Spirit to be present and just listen. We are asked to seek, knock and refuse to engage in an inner dialogue with our distractions. Bring stillness to the heart and just listen. Listening prayer is not God trusting us to listen; rather it is us trusting that God is present beyond the words (or in the words) waiting to bask in our attention. It is simply being still and waiting, being attentive and open to the Holy Spirit.

When we can effectively turn our attention from distractions to Jesus, we become more attentive. The quieter our hearts can enter into centering and stillness, our active listening skills switch on.

Listening Prayer turns us away from elaborate internal commentaries, noisy inner chaos and catastrophic thinking. Encouraging us to listen to a voice that is not our own. A rule of thumb I use is, if it sounds like me, it's probably me. If it sounds pure, peaceful and sincere, however, it is God.

Developing an ear that recognizes God's voice and that listens to your life opens up the possibility of hearing from God through anyone or anything. Practice listening to God and you will develop a heart tuned to the pitch and timbre of God's word to you.

This practice builds intimacy in your relationship with God.

Revelation 3:20 The Passion

Behold, I'm standing at the door, knocking. If your heart is open to hear my voice and you open the door within, I will come in to you and feast with you, and you will feast with me.

Journal:

What came up for you while reading this devotion? How can you practice active listening today? What will you take forward and think about today?

Morning Prayer:

Help me quietly learn and listen. Amen.

Nourishment:

Enjoy a cup of lemon water to prepare your body for the day.

Movement:

Standing in Mountain Position, interlace your fingers behind your back. Roll the shoulders to the back body and tilt the chin to the ceiling. Take three cleansing breaths over the front side of the heart. This allows the tension to roll off our shoulders while opening the heart and throat chakras.

Day 1 Evening

Nourishment:

Enjoying a cup of hot lemon water to help slow down your body and mind for restoration.

Slowing the movement:

From a comfortable reclined restorative position, place both hands on the belly. Recognize the rise and fall of the breath. Relax in silence for a minimum of 2 minutes.

Silence, stillness and centering on:
I am calm. I am peaceful. I am attentive.

Devotional:

Psalm 119:105 NASB

Your word is a lamp to my feet and a light to my path.

When I am seeking direction on a circumstance in my life, I will pray for a scripture or a word. His Word truly is the lamp to my feet and the light of my path. I have stirred myself wrong, His word has not let me down. I also noticed that to assure me, he doesn't just send the word or the scripture once, it is noticeably dropped in my path to give me the light I need.

Recently, I was seeking direction on a circumstance in my life. I was at a crossroad, having to make a choice and needing to know that God was with me. I had prayed the night before for some kind of a sign. He woke me at 4:33 and I knew instinctively that it was a scripture I needed to read Philippians 4:33 which says I can do all things through Christ who strengthens me. I do a prayer walk after my morning devotions and yoga, as I was walking a feather floated down out of nowhere and got my attention. Feathers for me have always been a sign of God or angels in my life, especially those feathers found in places randomly. Living a spirit lead life and walking close to God letting his word be the lamp to my feet and a light to my path has been a much more peaceful and content life than I have ever lived. Developing that intimacy with God you will begin to see him everywhere. When you trust His guidance in your life he will light your path.

Journal:

Review your day. How have you been able to create space in the body, mind and soul to let God light your path today? Where did you see God's word today? Journal those things you are thankful for and things you remain hopeful of.

Additional journal prompts for overall health and wellness:
~nourishment
~movement

Pray.

Day 2 Morning

Find a comfortable restorative pose, one hand on heart one hand on belly recognizing the breath as it flows through the body. Enjoy the silence and calmness for at least 2 minutes, paying attention to the breath, the gentle rise and fall of the chest and belly.

Silence, stillness and centering for a minimum of 2 minutes on:
I am calm. I am peaceful. I am attentive.

Devotional reading:

To engage in holy listening we need to prepare ourselves by:

Sharpening our active listening skills;
Finding the quietness at our heart centre;
Distinguishing our voice from God's voice;
Trusting God to speak in His own time;
Engaging and inviting Him into the prayer, letting him know you are listening.

1 Samuel 3:10

Speak, Lord, for your servant is listening.

Journal:

What came up for you while reading this devotion? How have you been engaging and inviting Him into your prayers? How can you listen more deeply?

Morning Prayer:

Help me quietly listen deeply today, show me what I can learn. Amen.

Nourishment:

Enjoy a cup of lemon water to prepare your body for the day.

Movement:

Standing in Mountain Position, interlace your fingers behind your back. Roll the shoulders to the back body and tilt the chin to the ceiling. Take three cleansing breaths over the front side of the heart. This allows the tension to roll off our shoulders while opening the heart and throat chakras.

Day 2 Evening

Nourishment:

Enjoying a cup of hot lemon water to help slow your body and mind down for restoration.

Slowing the movement:

From a comfortable reclined restorative position, place both hands on the belly. Recognize the rise and fall of the breath. Relax in silence for a minimum of 2 minutes.

Silence, stillness and centering on:
I am calm. I am peaceful. I am attentive.

Devotional:

John 10:27 The Voice

My sheep respond as they hear My voice; I know them intimately, and they follow Me.

As we become comfortable with the quieting and the listening practise, there is such great comfort in being one of His sheep. The intimacy found in relationship with God is the most comforting feeling I have ever felt. Once that intimacy is established and nurtured we realize that there is so much grace in the love that He has for us. Thing is, we are all sinners, we have been born both saint and sinner. The atoning sacrifice of Jesus gave us the grace that allows us to faithfully put one foot in front of the other.

Journal:

Review your day. How have you been able to create space in the body, mind and soul to be a better active listener? Where was it comfortable to listen and where was it uncomfortable? Journal those things you are thankful for and things you remain hopeful of.

Additional journal prompts for overall health and wellness:
~nourishment
~movement

Pray.

Day 3 Morning

Find a comfortable restorative pose, one hand on heart one hand on belly recognizing the breath as it flows through the body. Enjoy the silence and calmness for at least 2 minutes, paying attention to the breath, the gentle rise and fall of the chest and belly.

Silence, stillness and centering for a minimum of 2 minutes on:
I am calm. I am peaceful. I am attentive.

Devotional reading:

Proverbs 2:2 AMP

So that your ear is attentive to (skillful and godly) wisdom,
And apply your heart to understanding (seeking it conscientiously and striving for it eagerly).

As I am reminded by my family roots in Romanian Orthodox tradition, we need to 'be attentive.' In all the services I have attended the Father encouraged us to 'be attentive' this phrase is sung several times throughout the service bringing our attention back to what he will sing or chant next.

Proverbs 2:6 goes on to say "the Lord gives (skillful and godly) wisdom; From His mouth come knowledge and understanding." That being said, our active listening skills are essential in our spiritual growth and development.

Journal:

What came up for you while reading this devotion? How can you be more attentive and welcome the invitation to listen more and talk less. Will it be easy or hard to listen more and talk less today?

Morning Prayer:

Help me quietly learn and listen. Amen.

Nourishment:

Enjoy a cup of lemon water to prepare your body for the day.

Movement:

Standing in Mountain Position, interlace your fingers behind your back. Roll the shoulders to the back body and tilt the chin to the ceiling. Take three cleansing breaths over the front side of the heart. This allows the tension to roll off our shoulders while opening the heart and throat chakras.

Day 3 Evening

Nourishment:

Enjoying a cup of hot lemon water to help slow down your body and mind for restoration.

Slowing the movement:

From a comfortable reclined restorative position, place both hands on the belly. Recognize the rise and fall of the breath. Relax in silence for a minimum of 2 minutes.

Silence, stillness and centering on:
I am calm. I am peaceful. I am attentive.

Devotional:

Ezekiel 3:10

Let all my words sink deeply into your own heart first. Listen to them carefully for yourself.

Let the words sink into your heart first! Love that! Listen with the ears of the heart. The heart space is central for actively listening to God's word. The scripture then goes on to explain that we should take those words out with us and tell others, whether they listen or not. The lamp that lights our feet can also be the encouragement for others.

Journal:

Review your day. How have you been able to create space in the body, mind and soul to be an attentive listener? Was listening hard or easy today? Journal those things you are thankful for and things you remain hopeful of.

Additional journal prompts for overall health and wellness:
~nourishment
~movement

Pray.

Day 4 Morning

Find a comfortable restorative pose, one hand on heart one hand on belly recognizing the breath as it flows through the body. Enjoy the silence and calmness for at least 2 minutes, paying attention to the breath, the gentle rise and fall of the chest and belly.

Silence, stillness and centering for a minimum of 2 minutes on:
I am calm. I am peaceful. I am attentive.

Devotional reading:

Silence is hard in a world where our lives are so busy and noisy! I have studied the spiritual discipline of silence and have found that the more busy and noisy our lives are, the more difficult it becomes to hear the soft whisper of the Holy Spirit speaking into our lives. Practicing silence helps us quiet our heart centre. From there, we can open ourselves up to holy listening. Our ability to listen helps us hear what God is saying to our hearts and lives. When we shut off our minds to the distractions and sounds of life to spend time alone with God we can better hear what He has to say.

In *Spiritual Disciplines Handbook – Practices That Transform Us*, Adele Ahberg Calhoun explains:

It is difficult to find silence in an age of technology and information. Silence challenges our cultural addiction to amusement, words, music, advertising, noise, alarms and voices. Silence asks for patience and waiting. And both silence and waiting make us uncomfortable. They seem so unproductive. We can't tell if we are doing anything in them. So when we come upon silence, we fill it. We cram it with something else we can learn or do or achieve....We need to realize that the world can go on without us for an hour or a day or even longer. We don't need to respond to every word and request that comes our way. The discipline of silence invites us to leave behind the competing demands of our outer world for time alone with Jesus. Silence offers a way of paying attention to the Spirit of God and what he brings to the surface of our souls.

In quietness we often notice things we would rather not notice or feel. Pockets of sadness or anger or loneliness or impatience begin to surface. Our own outer agenda looms larger than our desire to be with God in silence. And as the silence settles in and nothing seems to be happening, we often struggle with the feeling that we are wasting time. Everything we notice in this struggle can become an invitation to prayer. Like a can opener, the silence opens up the contents of our heart, allowing us deeper access to God than we experience at other times. As we remain in silence, the inner noise and chaos will begin to settle. Our capacity to open up wider and wider to God grows. The Holy One has access to places we don't even know exist.

Jesus told his disciples, "I have much more to say to you, more than you can now bear" (John 16:12). It is the Holy Spirit's job to keep the inner process of revelation underway. But in order for the Spirit to do his job, we need to cooperate and put ourselves in a place to deeply and reflectively listen. Be alone with God in the silence. Offer your body and your attention to God as a prayer.

As you quietly offer your body, you can hone your listening reflexes. There is nothing you need to do here. This is not a time to come up with strategies for fixing your life. Silence is a time to rest in God. Lean into God, trusting that being with him in silence will loosen your rootedness in the world and plant you by the streams of living water. It can form your life even if it doesn't solve your life.

For me silence with God is a way of life, let him uproot you today and plant you by the streams of living water! My time spent in silence leads to prayer, leads to my time with God and allows me to hear what he has to say or show me.

Journal:

What came up for you while reading this devotion? Where can you loosen your rootedness and trade chaos for silence to listen? Where can you make room in your day to cooperate with the Spirit?

Morning Prayer:

Help me quietly learn and listen. Amen.

Nourishment:

Enjoy a cup of lemon water to prepare your body for the day.

Movement:

Standing in Mountain Position, interlace your fingers behind your back. Roll the shoulders to the back body and tilt the chin to the ceiling. Take three cleansing breaths over the front side of the heart. This allows the tension to roll off our shoulders while opening the heart and throat chakras.

Day 4 Evening

Nourishment:

Enjoying a cup of hot lemon water to help slow your body and mind down for restoration.

Slowing the movement:

From a comfortable reclined restorative position, place both hands on the belly. Recognize the rise and fall of the breath. Relax in silence for a minimum of 2 minutes.

Silence, stillness and centering on:
I am calm. I am peaceful. I am attentive.

Devotional:

Proverbs 3:5-6 The Message

Trust God from the bottom of your heart;
Don't try to figure out everything on your own.
Listen for God's voice in everything you do,
everywhere you go;
He's the one who will keep you on track.

Listen to the stirring in your heart, recognize where God's voice shows up for you.

Journal:

Review your day. How have you been able to create space in the body, mind and soul for trusting and recognizing his voice today? Where was God speaking to you today? Journal those things you are thankful for and things you remain hopeful of.

Additional journal prompts for overall health and wellness:
~nourishment
~movement

Pray.

Day 5 Morning

Find a comfortable restorative pose, one hand on heart one hand on belly recognizing the breath as it flows through the body. Enjoy the silence and calmness for at least 2 minutes, paying attention to the breath, the gentle rise and fall of the chest and belly.

Silence, stillness and centering for a minimum of 2 minutes on:
I am calm. I am peaceful. I am attentive.

Devotional reading:

Matthew 6:25-34 The Voice

Jesus says: Here is the bottom line: do not worry about your life. Don't worry about what you will eat or what you will drink. Don't worry about how you clothe your body. Living is about more than merely eating, and the body is about more than dressing up. Look at the birds in the sky. They do not store food for the winter. They don't plant gardens. They do not sow or reap – and yet, they are always fed because your heavenly Father feeds them. And you are even more precious to Him than a beautiful bird. If He looks after them, of course He will look after you. Worrying does not do any good; who can claim to add even an hour to his life by worrying?

Nor should you worry about clothes. Consider the lilies of the field and how they grow. They do not work or weave or sew, and yet their garments are stunning. Even King Solomon, dressed in his most regal garb, was not as lovely as these lilies. And think about grassy fields – the grasses are here now, but they will be dead by winter. And yet God adorns them so radiantly. How much more will He clothe you, you of little faith, you have not trust?

So do not consume yourselves with questions: What will we eat? What will be drink? What will we wear? Outsiders make themselves frantic over such questions; they do not realize that your heavenly Father knows exactly what you need. Seek first the kingdom of God and His righteousness, and then all these things will be given to you too. So do not worry about tomorrow. Let tomorrow worry about itself. Living faithfully is a large enough task for today.

I love how Jesus bottom lines it! I love the words written in red. How can you lean in and listen to Jesus more today?

Journal:

What came up for you while reading this devotion? Where can you add more of God's peace and resist worry in your day? How can you manage to listen and trust him more with your daily routine?

Morning Prayer:

May I live faithfully today. Amen.

Nourishment:

Enjoy a cup of lemon water to prepare your body for the day.

Movement:

Standing in Mountain Position, interlace your fingers behind your back. Roll the shoulders to the back body and tilt the chin to the ceiling. Take three cleansing breaths over the front side of the heart. This allows the tension to roll off our shoulders while opening the heart and throat chakras.

Day 5 Evening

Nourishment:

Enjoying a cup of hot lemon water to help slow your body and mind down for restoration.

Slowing the movement:

From a comfortable reclined restorative position, place both hands on the belly. Recognize the rise and fall of the breath. Relax in silence for a minimum of 2 minutes.

Silence, stillness and centering on:
I am calm. I am peaceful. I am attentive.

Devotional:

When we talk about the inner movement of our hearts, that is the Holy Spirit spurring us on. One can choose to receive it or ignore it. When we read certain passages or hear certain songs or stories, God uses those opportunities to stir our heart. When God stirs the heart the Spirit is willing. That is our invitation to accept His joy, peace and love in our lives. The vibration within our bodies when we feel that stirring is an incredible healing energy. When we participate with the indwelling of the Holy Spirit, together with the energy flowing in our bodies, we are taking on the characteristics of Jesus and we become a willing participant to live a grace-filled life. A grace-filled life offers healing in and through our bodies.

2 Timothy 1:7 Amplified Bible

For God did not give us a spirit of timidity or cowardice or fear, but (He has given us a spirit) of power and love and of sound judgment and personal discipline (abilities that result in a calm, well-balanced mind and self-control).

Journal:

Take time to reflect on this devotion. Discuss what, if anything, came up during this reflection. What benefits are you already recognizing after five days of focusing on the listening with the ears of the heart?

What has stirred your heart the most? Check in with: body, mind, soul and strength. Be honest!

Additional journal prompts for overall health and wellness:
~nourishment
~movement

Pray.

In this segment we developed our holy listening. We looked at ways to loosen our rootedness in the world and root ourselves by streams of living waters. This allows the word of God to rule deeply in our hearts so that we might find his peace (adapted from Colossians 3:15). Colossians 3:15 essentially reminds us to just breathe. To find that inner calm as we walk with Him daily. To understand where and how God speaks with you. Silence is the space for listening. However, silence can be uncomfortable at first. Learning to be comfortable in the uncomfortable builds our endurance. That endurance will build your Christ-like characteristics. As we become more like Jesus we will develop better listening skills. This is a practice which you need to personalize. I can only speak to the practices that guided my spiritual growth. I encourage you to find a listening practice that speaks to your heart and your personality and becomes your road map.

At times you will find your anxious thoughts and worries will get in the way of your ability to listen. I offer a prayer that has helped me when I fear things have gone quiet:

Psalm 139 The Passion

God, I invite your searching gaze into my heart. Examine me through and through, find out everything that may be hidden within me. Put me to the test and sift through all my anxious cares. See if there is any path of pain I'm walking on and lead me back to your glorious, everlasting ways - the path that brings me back to you. Amen

SEGMENT 6

~

Restoring

"We may ignore, but we can nowhere evade, the Presence of God. The world is crowded with Him. He walks everywhere incognito."

- C.S. Lewis

Over the course of my journey I have learned that Jesus changes everything! At one of my Holy Yoga retreats we focused on the fact that as we soften our gaze and pay more attention, we allow the eyes of our heart to see and hear. We then receive a holy invitation to recognize the Spirit of God and encounter God in all areas of our journey.

He is the peace that passes all human understanding. He is a place of rest and restoration. When he knocks and we let him in we feast on restoration that can only be only found in Him and the peace which he brings.

Once you find that peace your body starts to restore and heal the broken bits on a deeper level.

Day 1 Morning

Find a comfortable restorative pose, one hand on heart one hand on belly recognizing the breath as it flows through the body. Enjoy the silence and calmness for at least 2 minutes, paying attention to the breath, the gentle rise and fall of the chest and belly.

Silence, stillness and centering for a minimum of 2 minutes on:
I am safe. I am happy. I am free.

Devotional reading:

Enforce Love – Ephesians 2:4-5

God is love and as you call down love you call down the heart of God himself, and you call down the power of His Kingdom.

The best way I can describe 'the power of His Kingdom' and our ability to 'call down the heart of God himself' is like advancing to the next level of a video game. The restoration our body gets and the growth we see in our spirituality is next level healing. The more you call down the love of God, His Holy Spirit and His Kingdom are walking with you everywhere you go. When that heart chakra and heart centre is constantly refueling on love energy, the healing is powerful.

Journal:

What came up for you while reading this devotion? Where can you call down the heart of God in your daily routine? What deeper level broken bits are you needing healed today?

Morning Prayer:

Holy Spirit you are welcome here. Amen.

Nourishment:

Enjoy a cup of lemon water to prepare your body for the day.

Movement:

Standing in Mountain Position, interlace your fingers behind your back. Roll the shoulders to the back body and tilt the chin to the ceiling. Take three cleansing breaths over the front side of the heart. This allows the tension to roll off our shoulders while opening the heart and throat chakras.

Day 1 Evening

Nourishment:

Enjoying a cup of hot lemon water to help slow down your body and mind for restoration.

Slowing the movement:

From a comfortable reclined restorative position, place both hands on the belly. Recognize the rise and fall of the breath. Relax in silence for a minimum of 2 minutes.

Silence, stillness and centering on:
I am safe. I am happy. I am free.

Devotional:

Psalm 37:7

Be still before the Lord and wait patiently for him;

Waiting patiently is not easy. Trying to stay in the present moment while waiting is difficult. I have found the following tips helpful when He has asked me to just wait longer:

(Adapted from *Spiritual Disciplines Handbook - Practices That Transform us,* Adele Ahlberg Calhoun)

While waiting:

- not imagining the worst case scenarios;
- stay in the present moment;
- not waiting on a future to which you can finally live;
- surrender your timetable to God;
- letting go of control;
- allowing others space and time to change;
- gracing your ownself with space and time to grow;
- trust that God's timing is the perfect timing.

Journal:

Review your day. How have you been able to create space in the body, mind and soul to be still and wait patiently on God today? Was finding restoration hard or easy today? Journal those things you are thankful for and things you remain hopeful of.

Additional journal prompts for overall health and wellness:
~nourishment
~movement

Pray.

Day 2 Morning

Find a comfortable restorative pose, one hand on heart one hand on belly recognizing the breath as it flows through the body. Enjoy the silence and calmness for at least 2 minutes, paying attention to the breath, the gentle rise and fall of the chest and belly.

Silence, stillness and centering for a minimum of 2 minutes on:
I am safe. I am happy. I am free.

Devotional reading:

Matthew 6:34 NLT

So don't worry about tomorrow, for tomorrow will bring its own worries. Today's trouble is enough for today.

Can you go the entire day not worrying? Here is a challenge: each time a worry sneaks into your mind, take a big inhale and on the exhale send that worry to God. Bring your mind space back to your heart space and be present in the current moment. The more you are able to do this the easier it gets, I promise you that!

Journal:

What came up for you while reading this devotion? Where can you call down the heart of God in your daily routine handing over your worries as they enter your mind? How can you intentionally exhale your worries to God?

Morning Prayer:

Lord, fill me with your refreshing inhale as I exhale all my worries and anxieties to you. Amen.

Nourishment:

Enjoy a cup of lemon water to prepare your body for the day.

Movement:

Standing in Mountain Position, interlace your fingers behind your back. Roll the shoulders to the back body and tilt the chin to the ceiling. Take three cleansing breaths over the front side of the heart. This allows the tension to roll off our shoulders while opening the heart and throat chakras.

Day 2 Evening

Nourishment:

Enjoying a cup of hot lemon water to help slow your body and mind down for restoration.

Slowing the movement:

From a comfortable reclined restorative position, place both hands on the belly. Recognize the rise and fall of the breath. Relax in silence for a minimum of 2 minutes.

Silence, stillness and centering on:
I am safe. I am happy. I am free.

Devotional:

As you breathe in, consider that you are breathing in God's Promises.

Micah 7:7 NASB

But as for me, I will watch expectantly for the Lord;
I will wait for the God of my salvation.
My God will hear me.

Journal:

Review your day. How have you been able to create space in the body, mind and soul to breathe in God's promises? Journal those things you are thankful for and things you remain hopeful of.

Additional journal prompts for overall health and wellness:
~nourishment
~movement

Pray.

Day 3 Morning

Find a comfortable restorative pose, one hand on heart one hand on belly recognizing the breath as it flows through the body. Enjoy the silence and calmness for at least 2 minutes, paying attention to the breath, the gentle rise and fall of the chest and belly.

Silence, stillness and centering for a minimum of 2 minutes on:
I am safe. I am happy. I am free.

Devotional reading:

Isaiah 26:2-7 The Voice

Now open the gates to welcome the righteous, so that those who keep faith may enter in.

You will keep the peace, a perfect peace, for all who trust in You, for those who dedicate their hearts and minds to You.

So trust in the Eternal One forever, for He is like a great Rock – strong, stable, trustworthy, and lasting.

When we can attach our anchor (dedicate our hearts and minds) to the Rock who is strong, stable, trustworthy and lasting, the rewards are a total transformation of the brain. As we learn to disengage the brain and allow it to sink into the heart space the brain gets to circulate in pure love. From that space of pure love we are able to trust in God. From that circular space of love and gratitude flows peace. And with His peace we have freedom!

Journal:

What came up for you while reading this devotion? Where can you add more of God's peace into your day? How can you manage to trust Him more with your daily routine?

Morning Prayer:

Lord, help me trust you more and make room for Your peace. Amen.

Nourishment:

Enjoy a cup of lemon water to prepare your body for the day.

Movement:

Standing in Mountain Position, interlace your fingers behind your back. Roll the shoulders to the back body and tilt the chin to the ceiling. Take three cleansing breaths over the front side of the heart. This allows the tension to roll off our shoulders while opening the heart and throat chakras.

Day 3 Evening

Nourishment:

Enjoying a cup of hot lemon water to help slow your body and mind down for restoration.

Slowing the movement:

From a comfortable reclined restorative position, place both hands on the belly. Recognize the rise and fall of the breath. Relax in silence for a minimum of 2 minutes.

Silence, stillness and centering on:
I am safe. I am happy. I am free.

Devotional:

> Philippians 4:6-7 TLB
>
> Don't worry about anything; instead, pray about everything; tell God your needs, and don't forget to thank him for his answers. If you do this, you will experience God's peace, which is far more wonderful than the human mind can understand. His peace will keep your thoughts and your hearts quiet and at rest as you trust in Christ Jesus.

When your mind returns to the place of worry, learning to bring that worry captive to God is the greatest tool in my spiritual tool box. When you catch yourself slipping into a worry, honestly praying about it is so much more refreshing for the body, mind and soul. I find that a phrase or even a word can let me release the grip I have on the worry and let it go. As you can tell by this point in the 40 day journey, there have been lots of prompts along the way to journal about being thankful for blessings received. I have also dedicated my prayer practice to include prayers of thanksgiving for those prayers that have been answered. I can tell you from my own experience that the peace offered through trusting Jesus is the best restoration my body, mind and soul has ever felt.

Journal:

Review your day. How have you been able to create space in the body, mind and soul to experience God's peace? Where can you exchange prayer for worry in your life today? Journal those things you are thankful for and things you remain hopeful of.

Additional journal prompts for overall health and wellness:
~nourishment
~movement

Pray.

Day 4 Morning

Find a comfortable restorative pose, one hand on heart one hand on belly recognizing the breath as it flows through the body. Enjoy the silence and calmness for at least 2 minutes, paying attention to the breath, the gentle rise and fall of the chest and belly.

Silence, stillness and centering for a minimum of 2 minutes on:
I am safe. I am happy. I am free.

Devotional reading:

The following scripture is very close to my heart. It is one that has kept coming up for me in different seasons of my life. When I meditate on this scripture I often get direction for things that I need to focus on or let go of. It helps me focus on living heaven on earth and keep a Kingdom mindset.

Ecclesiastes 3:1-15

For everything that happens in life – there is a season, a right time for everything under heaven:

A time to be born, a time to die;
a time to plant, a time to collect the harvest;
A time to kill, a time to heal;
a time to tear down, a time to build up;
A time to cry, a time to laugh;
a time to mourn, a time to dance;
A time to scatter stones, a time to pile them up;

a time for a warm embrace, a time for keeping your
   distance;
A time to search, a time to give up as lost;
a time to keep, a time to throw out;
A time to tear apart, a time to bind together;
a time to be quiet, a time to speak up;
A time to love, a time to hate;
a time to go to war, a time to make peace.

What good comes to anyone who works so hard,
all to gain a few possessions? I have seen the kinds
of tasks God has given each of us to do to keep
one busy, and I know God has made everything
beautiful for its time. God has also placed in our
minds a sense of eternity; we look back on the
past and ponder over the future, yet we cannot
understand the doings of God. I know there is
nothing better for us than to be joyful and to do
good throughout our lives; to eat and drink and
see the good in all of our hard work is a gift from
God. I know everything God does endures for all
time. Nothing can be added to it; nothing can be
taken away from it. We humans can only stand in
awe of all God has done. What has been and what
is to be – already is. And God holds accountable all
pursuits of humanity.

This scripture reminds us that our human lives and earthly accomplishments are fleeting. Nothing tangible is permanent. No work lasts. It all slips away and vanishes into thin air. Now compare that to God. Everything God does is substantial. Everything God accomplishes lasts forever. Every word God speaks makes a difference. And so, God places within every person a sense of eternity to know yet not understand Him. This world with all its goodness and beauty is not as good as it gets. There is more, so much more, and we are made for that reality too.

Journal:

As you read this scripture what stirred your heart? Where can you focus more on living heaven on earth rather than the fleeting things this world has to offer? How can you focus more on the gifts of God?

Morning Prayer:

Lord, help me trust you more and make room for Your peace. Amen.

Nourishment:

Enjoy a cup of lemon water to prepare your body for the day.

Movement:

Standing in Mountain Position, interlace your fingers behind your back. Roll the shoulders to the back body and tilt the chin to the ceiling. Take three cleansing breaths over the front side of the heart. This allows the tension to roll off our shoulders while opening the heart and throat chakras.

Day 4 Evening

Nourishment:

Enjoying a cup of hot lemon water to help slow your body and mind down for restoration.

Slowing the movement:

From a comfortable reclined restorative position, place both hands on the belly. Recognize the rise and fall of the breath. Relax in silence for a minimum of 2 minutes.

Silence, stillness and centering on:
I am safe. I am happy. I am free.

Devotional:

Without a doubt there is a reason and a season for everything in our lives. It is important to realize that God will meet you in every situation if you invite him in. As difficult as some situations may get, choose to anchor yourself to God. That way, when the winds of change try to rearrange, you can trust that God will bring calm to the storm and meet you exactly where you are.

> Even when it hurts
> Even when it is hard
> Even when it all just falls apart
> I will run to You
> 'Cause I know that You are
> Lover of my soul
> Healer of my scars
> You steady my heart

> \- Kari Jobe (taken from Julie
> Clinton's Be Fearless)

Journal:

Review your day. How have you been able to create space in the body, mind and soul to experience God's peace in your current season? Are you willing to let the Lord heal your scars? Journal those things you are thankful for and things of which you remain hopeful.

Additional journal prompts for overall health and wellness:
~nourishment
~movement

Pray.

Day 5 Morning

Find a comfortable restorative pose, one hand on heart one hand on belly recognizing the breath as it flows through the body. Enjoy the silence and calmness for at least 2 minutes, paying attention to the breath, the gentle rise and fall of the chest and belly.

Silence, stillness and centering for a minimum of 2 minutes on:
I am safe. I am happy. I am free.

Devotional reading:

Isaiah 40:31 The Voice

But those who trust in the Eternal One will regain
    their strength.
They will soar on wings as eagles.
They will run – never winded, never weary.
They will walk – never tired, never faint.

This is a reminder that when we wait on the Lord we need to lean into his restoration. As we soar on the wings of eagles, it brings us closer to God. Take the time to enjoy waiting longer. Remember that God's signature on events is timing and as you wait, live expectantly knowing that His timing is the best timing!

Journal:

As you read this scripture did it empower you to wait in the circumstances you are waiting for? Can you visualize yourself soaring like an eagle? How can you manage to trust him more with your daily routine?

Morning Prayer:

Lord, help me trust you more and make room for Your peace. Amen.

Nourishment:

Enjoy a cup of lemon water to prepare your body for the day.

Movement:

Standing in Mountain Position, interlace your fingers behind your back. Roll the shoulders to the back body

and tilt the chin to the ceiling. Take three cleansing breaths over the front side of the heart. This allows the tension to roll off our shoulders while opening the heart and throat chakras.

Day 5 Evening

Nourishment:

Enjoying a cup of hot lemon water to help slow your body and mind down for restoration.

Slowing the movement:

From a comfortable reclined restorative position, place both hands on the belly. Recognize the rise and fall of the breath. Relax in silence for a minimum of 2 minutes.

Silence, stillness and centering on:
I am safe. I am happy. I am free.

Devotional:

Psalm 86:15-17 The Passion

But Lord, your nurturing love is tender and gentle. You are slow to get angry yet swift to show your faithful love.

You are full of abounding grace and truth.
Bring me to your grace-fountain
So that your strength becomes mine.
Be my hero and come rescue your servant once
     again!
Send me a miraculous sign to show me how much
     you love me…

What I have learned is that God is okay with us jumping up on the mercy seat. Asking him to be our hero, asking for a sign of his love in our lives. He desires us to have an intimate relationship with Him. He offers only nurturing, tender and gentle love.

Journal:

Review your day. How have you been able to create space in the body, mind and soul to experience the restoration of God's love when we learn to receive his grace and trust in Him? Journal those things you are thankful for and things you remain hopeful of.

Additional journal prompts for overall health and wellness:
~nourishment
~movement

Pray.

In this segment we took an indepth look at restoration. As we restore we allow peace to set into our body, mind and souls to heal the broken bits at a deeper level. We allow God to be the tour guide of our spiritual journey. Our relationship with the Triune (Father, Son and Holy Spirit) changes everything. We begin to realize that the presence of God is everywhere and as C.S. Lewis says 'He walks everywhere incognito'.

As we learn to soften our gaze and pay more attention we can see more clearly with the eyes of the heart. And with the clearer vision we can begin to achieve a higher level of healing and a higher level of spiritual growth. You will begin to experience the power of the Holy Spirit in so many wonderful ways. God truly does walk incognito everywhere and experiencing that has been a sensational gift in my life. Becoming a prayer warrior has also been an enriching gift in my spiritual life.

As a prayer warrior, I love reading stories about Daniel and his fasting and praying techniques. I know first hand that devout praying gets things done. Prayer changes everything! When you can get a group of people to pray the same prayer it really does move mountains.

Daniel 2:19-23 The Voice

Then, one night, the mystery was revealed to Daniel in a vision, and so Daniel offered this blessing to the God of heaven:

Daniel: Praise the name of God forever and ever.
　　For all wisdom and power belong to Him.
　　He sets in motion the times and the ages;
　　He deposes kings and installs others;
　　He gives wisdom to the wise
　　And grants knowledge to those with understanding.
　　He reveals deep truths and hidden secrets;
　　He knows what lies veiled in the darkness;
　　Pure light radiates from within Him.
　　I recognize who You are, and I praise You, God of my ancestors,
　　For You have given me wisdom and strength.

Let your prayers make a difference on your journey and in your circle of love and your community. My own prayer life was really bland before I started on this journey. As I look back, it is amazing to see the ways in which the Holy Spirit has pruned me to become the prayer warrior I am today.

As we move from the cultivated soil of restoration to growing I leave you with a favorite prayer of mine which is The Prayer of David:

Psalm 16:11 The Voice

Instead, You direct me on the path that leads to a beautiful life. As I walk with You, the pleasures are never-ending, and I know true joy and contentment.

This prayer of David has become a daily prayer of mine. It is true as we walk closer to Jesus and lean into him more, the pleasures are never-ending. It is a spot of true joy and contentment. When I feel like I am not feeling all of these things, I bring it back to this simple prayer and I am able to get my head space into my heart space. It truly helps me open the ears of my heart!

~

Growing

Pain and suffering change us. When we are able to soften our gaze upon our brokenness and when we can look at that brokenness through Jesus' eyes we can allow our light within to grow stronger. This allows the pain and suffering of our past to change us in a positive way. Fueling up on kindness, peace and love sends healing energy to all areas of our body, mind and soul. That energy allows us to heal our brokenness and the light within us helps others grow and heal too.

I have seen it in my own family and the families of those I have counseled or mentored through the pain and suffering of their brokenness. As we vibrate on higher frequencies the spillover of that energy showers others with kindness, peace and love. The more we grow and plant seeds in our families and communities the more likely it is that those seeds get cultivated and grow stronger.

We can help others through our own testimonies and trials of our own journeys.

Day 1 Morning

Find a comfortable restorative pose, one hand on heart one hand on belly recognizing the breath as it flows through the body. Enjoy the silence and calmness for at least 2 minutes, paying attention to the breath, the gentle rise and fall of the chest and belly.

Silence, stillness and centering for a minimum of 2 minutes on:
I am faithful. I am patient. I am prayerful.

Devotional reading:

2 Peter 1:3-8 The Passion

God's Generous Grace
Everything we could ever need for life and complete devotion to God has already been deposited in us by his divine power. For all this was lavished upon us through the rich experience of knowing him who has called us by name and invited us to come to him through the power of these tremendous promises you can experience partnership with the divine nature, by which you have escaped the corrupt desires that are of the world.

Faith's Ladder of Virtue

So devote yourselves to lavishly supplementing your faith with goodness,

> and to goodness add understanding,
> and to understanding add the strength of self-control,
> and to self-control add patient endurance,
> and to patient endurance add godliness,
> and to godliness add mercy toward your brothers and sisters,
> and to mercy toward others add unending love.

Since these virtues are already planted deep within, and you possess them in abundant supply, they will keep you from being inactive or fruitless in your pursuit of knowing Jesus Christ more intimately. The more intimately we know Jesus the greater our ability to demonstrate our Christlike characteristics.

Journal:

What came up for you while reading this devotion? Where are you on Faith's ladder of virtue? With God's help, what do you need to work on today?

Morning Prayer:

Lord help the love and goodness you planted in me grow and grow, each and every day. Amen.

Nourishment:

Enjoy a cup of lemon water to prepare your body for the day.

Movement:

Standing in Mountain Position, interlace your fingers behind your back. Roll your shoulders to the back body and tilt your chin to the ceiling. Take three cleansing breaths over the front side of the heart. This allows the tension to roll off our shoulders while opening the heart and throat chakras.

Day 1 Evening

Nourishment:

Enjoying a cup of hot lemon water to help slow down your body and mind for restoration.

Slowing the movement:

From a comfortable reclined restorative position, place both hands on the belly. Recognize the rise and fall of the breath. Relax in silence for a minimum of 2 minutes.

Silence, stillness and centering on:
I am willing. I am growing. I am content.

Devotional:

Psalm 118:29 The Passion

So let's keep on giving our thanks to God, for he is so good!
His constant, tender love lasts forever!

An essential component to spiritual growth is giving thanks to God, while knowing his tender love is dependable, consistent and lasts forever. When we can start our days and end our days circulating in love and thanksgiving, the healing powers are dynamic.

Journal:

Review your day. How have you been able to create space in the body, mind and soul to grow your faith in God today? Reflecting upon your day, where were you able to bring your thoughts captive to love and thanksgiving? Journal those things you are thankful for and things you remain hopeful of.

Additional journal prompts for overall health and wellness:
~nourishment
~movement

Pray.

Day 2 Morning

Find a comfortable restorative pose, one hand on heart one hand on belly recognizing the breath as it flows through the body. Enjoy the silence and calmness for at least 2 minutes, paying attention to the breath, the gentle rise and fall of the chest and belly.

Silence, stillness and centering for a minimum of 2 minutes on:
I am faithful. I am patient. I am prayerful.

Devotional reading:

Proverbs 3:3 The Living Bible

Never tire of loyalty and kindness. Hold these virtues tightly. Write them deep within your heart.

I love this version of Proverbs 3:3. It comes alive for me with the "loyalty and kindness." Those are important elements for our journey to be the light bearer of God's word. Live a good life in the eyes of God and the eyes of those around you. Be a passionate ambassador of God's love throughout your everyday interactions with those he has placed in your life and in your reach.

Journal:

What came up for you while reading this devotion? Where can you hold tight to the virtues of being loyal and kind? How can you not lose grip of love and loyalty in your relationships?

Morning Prayer:

Lord help kindness and loyalty sink deep into my heart. Amen.

Nourishment:

Enjoy a cup of lemon water to prepare your body for the day.

Movement:

Standing in Mountain Position, interlace your fingers behind your back. Roll your shoulders to the back body and tilt your chin to the ceiling. Take three cleansing breaths over the front side of the heart. This allows the tension to roll off our shoulders while opening the heart and throat chakras.

Day 2 Evening

Nourishment:

Enjoying a cup of hot lemon water to help slow down your body and mind for restoration.

Slowing the movement:

From a comfortable reclined restorative position, place both hands on the belly. Recognize the rise and fall of the breath. Relax in silence for a minimum of 2 minutes.

Silence, stillness and centering on:
I am willing. I am growing. I am content.

Devotional:

Proverbs 3:5 The Message

Trust God from the bottom of your heart;
Don't try to figure out everything on your own.

Listen for God's voice in everything you do, everywhere you go;
He's the one who will keep you on track.

Surrendering all of who we are — right to the bottom of our heart — and placing everything in God's hands and completely trusting him. As we grow in Christ we begin to hear God's voice in everything we do and everywhere we go. He is truly the one that keeps us on track.

Journal:

Review your day. How have you been able to create space in the body, mind and soul to allow God to keep you on track? Where did you hear God's voice today? Journal those things you are thankful for and things you remain hopeful of.

Additional journal prompts for overall health and wellness:
~nourishment
~movement

Pray.

Day 3 Morning

Find a comfortable restorative pose, one hand on heart one hand on belly recognizing the breath as it flows through the body. Enjoy the silence and calmness for at least 2 minutes, paying attention to the breath, the gentle rise and fall of the chest and belly.

Silence, stillness and centering for a minimum of 2 minutes on:
I am faithful. I am patient. I am prayerful.

Devotional reading:

James 3:17-18 AMP

Wisdom from above is first pure (morally and spiritually undefiled), then peace-loving (courteous, considerate), gentle, reasonable (and willing to listen), full of compassion and good fruits. It is unwavering, without (self-righteous) hypocrisy (and self-serving guile). And the seed whose fruit is righteous (spiritual maturity) is sown in peace by those who make peace (by actively encouraging goodwill between individuals).

James 3:17-18 The Passion

Wisdom from above is always pure, filled with peace, considerate and teachable. It is filled with love and never displays prejudice or hypocrisy in any form and it always bears the beautiful harvest of righteousness! Good seeds of wisdom's fruit will be planted with peaceful acts by those who cherish making peace.

James 3:17-18 The Voice

Heavenly wisdom centers on purity, peace, gentleness, deference, mercy, and other good fruits untainted by hypocrisy. The seed that flowers into righteousness will always be planted in peace by those who embrace peace.

When I am instructing a yoga class, I take the students through a prayerful refreshing of the body, mind and soul during the concluding meditation. One of the refreshing prayers is the reminder that wisdom from above is pure, peaceful and sincere. Wisdom from heaven brings joy to your body. It makes the body feel good! As we grow spiritually we are able to discern heaven's wisdom from the wisdom found in our own stinkin' thinkin' brains. The more we can bring our mind space to our heart space, the easier it is to release the stinkin' thinkin' as soon as it shows up. I find it helpful when my mind space wants to fly off somewhere other than the heart space to recite a scripture or simple text or word. As you become more aware of your triggers, you can train the brain to switch off the stinkin' thinkin' and bring those thoughts captive to the love God placed in your heart.

Journal:

What came up for you while reading this devotion? Where can you focus more on heavenly wisdom as you walk through this day? Where can you embrace peace and plant seeds of righteousness in your relationships and interactions today?

Morning Prayer:

Wisdom from above is pure, peaceful and sincere. Amen.

Nourishment:

Enjoy a cup of lemon water to prepare your body for the day.

Movement:

Standing in Mountain Position, interlace your fingers behind your back. Roll your shoulders to the back body and tilt your chin to the ceiling. Take three cleansing breaths over the front side of the heart. This allows the tension to roll off our shoulders while opening the heart and throat chakras.

Day 3 Evening

Nourishment:

Enjoying a cup of hot lemon water to help slow down your body and mind for restoration.

Slowing the movement:

From a comfortable reclined restorative position, place both hands on the belly. Recognize the rise and fall of the breath. Relax in silence for a minimum of 2 minutes.

Silence, stillness and centering on:
I am willing. I am growing. I am content.

Devotional:

Proverbs 2:10 NASB

For wisdom will enter your heart
And knowledge will be pleasant to your soul

This scripture is so incredibly refreshing. Read it slowly a few times and allow it to be absorbed body, mind and soul. I assert that our bodies know the truth and that is why heavenly knowledge is so refreshing and pleasant to our souls.

Journal:

Review your day. How have you been able to create space in the body, mind and soul to allow God to refresh you with His wisdom? Journal those things you are thankful for and those for which you remain hopeful.

Additional journal prompts for overall health and wellness:
~nourishment
~movement

Pray.

Day 4 Morning

Find a comfortable restorative pose, one hand on heart one hand on belly recognizing the breath as it flows through the body. Enjoy the silence and calmness for at least 2 minutes, paying attention to the breath, the gentle rise and fall of the chest and belly.

Silence, stillness and centering for a minimum of 2 minutes on:
I am faithful. I am patient. I am prayerful.

Devotional reading:

We are meant to take what we have learned, the wisdom we have received from above, to the streets. As a Holy Yoga International yoga instructor we are trained to take the Gospel to the ends of the earth. Never tire of being that light that spreads the Word in the things we say and do.

Ezekiel 3:10-11 The Living Bible

Son of dust, let my words sink deep into your own heart first; listen to them carefully for yourself. Then, afterward, go to your people and whether or not they will listen, tell them: "This is what the Lord God says!"

Matthew 6: 22 The Living Bible

Jesus says: If your eye is pure, there will be sunshine in your soul.

Romans 13:12 The Voice

...so walk out on your old dark life and put on the armour of light. May we all act as good and respectable people, living today the same way as we will in the day of His coming.

For me this is where my spirituality and my relationship with Jesus blossoms. As I have mentioned in the beginning of this book, I shudder when people refer to me as religious. Yes, my black sheep church in the neighbourhood I grew up in stirs my heart. It has an 'at home' feel for me, yet that wasn't always the case. The dogmatic approach to theology pushed me away from my childhood friend Jesus. Until my vertical was realigned and I got to reacquaint myself with my friend Jesus my life started to change. I agree that we need community and we need to be around other like-minded people to grow our relationship in Christ yet I understand the church setting is not for everyone. Where I am today my Church sparks my heart, I now hear with the ears of my heart and I get a distinct message from God each time I attend. Having that kind of connection with the Triune God, helps me cultivate the beautiful soul within me. As much as I say "Jesus is coming, look busy" to be silly, it does strike a deep chord for me. I assert that regardless of the church you attend or do not attend, it comes down to the relationship you have with God and how you cultivate that within your heart. And, if you can put on the armour of light, walk His walk and talk His talk, the sunshine in your soul can set free his nondogmatic truth of peace and love to help heal all those He has sent to be in your circle of love.

Journal:

What came up for you while reading this devotion? Where can you focus more on heavenly wisdom as you walk through this day? Where can you embrace peace and plant seeds of righteousness in your relationships and interactions today?

Morning Prayer:

Lord let the sunshine in my soul be light for all those who need your light today. Amen.

Nourishment:

Enjoy a cup of lemon water to prepare your body for the day.

Movement:

Standing in Mountain Position, interlace your fingers behind your back. Roll your shoulders to the back body and tilt your chin to the ceiling. Take three cleansing breaths over the front side of the heart. This allows the tension to roll off our shoulders while opening the heart and throat chakras.

Day 4 Evening

Nourishment:

Enjoying a cup of hot lemon water to help slow down your body and mind for restoration.

Slowing the movement:

From a comfortable reclined restorative position, place both hands on the belly. Recognize the rise and fall of the breath. Relax in silence for a minimum of 2 minutes.

Silence, stillness and centering on:
I am willing. I am growing. I am content.

Devotional:

1 Peter 3:4 AMP

Let it be (the inner beauty of) the hidden person of the heart, with imperishable quality and unfading charm of a gentle and peaceful spirit, (one that is calm and self-controlled, not overanxious, but serene and spiritually mature) which is precious in the sight of God.

I love how this scripture is so calming and soothing for the soul. Read it through a few times and let it refresh your soul and may you feel the gentle and peaceful spirit within you.

Journal:

Review your day. How have you been able to create space in the body, mind and soul to allow God to keep you on track? What is holding you back or spurring you on? Journal those things you are thankful for and things you remain hopeful of.

Additional journal prompts for overall health and wellness:
~nourishment
~movement

Pray.

Day 5 Morning

Find a comfortable restorative pose, one hand on heart one hand on belly recognizing the breath as it flows through the body. Enjoy the silence and calmness for at least 2 minutes, paying attention to the breath, the gentle rise and fall of the chest and belly.

Silence, stillness and centering for a minimum of 2 minutes on:
I am faithful. I am patient. I am prayerful.

Devotional reading:

Romans 12:11-13 The Voice

Do not slack in your faithfulness and hard work. Let your spirit be on fire, bubbling up and boiling over, as you serve the Lord. Do not forget to rejoice, for hope is always just around the corner. Hold up through the hard times that are coming, and devote yourselves to prayer. Share what you have with the saints, so they lack nothing; take every opportunity to open your life and home to others.

Whatever it is you do, do it to the best of your ability. As we go about our daily routines prayerfully and overflowing with joy, hope and faithfulness, it produces positive vibrations and that love-charged energy flows into everything we do and say. It blesses our lives and the lives of those around us.

Journal:

What came up for you while reading this devotion? Where can you be more prayerful and faithful in your daily routine? Where can you bubble up and boil over as you serve the Lord within your relationships and interactions today?

Morning Prayer:

Let me be joyful, hopeful, patient in all circumstances and faithful to you Lord. Amen.

Nourishment:

Enjoy a cup of lemon water to prepare your body for the day.

Movement:

Standing in Mountain Position, interlace your fingers behind your back. Roll your shoulders to the back body and tilt your chin to the ceiling. Take three cleansing breaths over the front side of the heart. This allows the tension to roll off our shoulders while opening the heart and throat chakras.

Day 5 Evening

Nourishment:

Enjoying a cup of hot lemon water to help slow down your body and mind for restoration.

Slowing the movement:

From a comfortable reclined restorative position, place both hands on the belly. Recognize the rise and fall of the breath. Relax in silence for a minimum of 2 minutes.

Silence, stillness and centering on:
I am willing. I am growing. I am content.

Devotional:

As we learned in this mornings devotion, let's try to:

Be joyful in hope,
Patient in affliction,
Faithful in prayer.

Growing spiritually is a continuous journey. Taking time to self-reflect on our Christ-like qualities transforms our lives and shapes our futures. Having consistent reminders at the end of the day is like a checklist of what God asked you to accomplish through your day. Meditating on this scripture has helped me immensely. Ending my day and asking myself, honestly, have I been joyful in hope? Why or why not? Where could I have been more patient? Was I faithful in prayer? Were there things I was reluctant to hand over to God? As your spiritual practise grows you will find what works best for you. Know that growth can be as simple as a short daily checklist.

Journal:

Review your day. How have you been able to create space in the body, mind and soul to allow God to keep you on track? Ask the Holy Spirit to help you with your personalized checklist. Journal those things you are thankful for and things you remain hopeful of.

Additional journal prompts for overall health and wellness:
~nourishment
~movement

Pray.

Segment 7 has been about growing. Acknowledging that pain and suffering change us and if we soften our gaze and embrace our Christ-like qualities we can take our past and reshape our future. We have discussed ways to create space in the body, mind and soul by building a daily routine that allows us to grow, bloom and flourish. Growing is a continuous lifelong process and, like a garden, it needs to be nurtured. If our growth gets stunted or stuck, our personal practise needs to give us that boost of nutrients when we need it. The following scriptures might be the boost your personal practise needs:

Matthew 13:31 The Voice

Jesus: The kingdom of heaven is like a mustard seed, which a sower took and planted in his field. Mustard seeds are minute, tiny – but the seeds grow into trees. Flocks of birds can come and build their nests in the branches.

As you read this scripture visualize the seed of love growing in your heart as you nurture it with the love of God. As we live in that love and cultivate that heart space our personal journey takes form. Your personal testimony and your journey to who you are today is living proof of God's love. As your faith grows and abundantly spills over, you are healing yourself and others on your walk.

1 Peter 1:22-25 NIV

Now that you have purified yourselves by obeying the truth so that you have sincere love for each other, love one another deeply, from the heart. For you have been born again, not of perishable seed, but of imperishable, through the living and enduring word of God. For, "All people are like grass, and all their glory is like the flowers of the field; the grass withers and the flowers fall, but the word of the Lord endures forever"

Take time to read this scripture and let it refresh your body, mind and soul.

1 John 1:5-9 TLB

God is Light and in him is no darkness at all. So if we say we are his friends but go on living in spiritual darkness and sin, we are lying. But if we are living in the light of God's presence, just as Christ does, then we have wonderful fellowship and joy with each other, and the blood of Jesus his Son cleanses us from every sin.

If we say that we have no sin, we are only fooling ourselves and refusing to accept the truth. But if we confess our sins to Him, He can be depended on to forgive us and to cleanse us from every wrong. And it is perfectly proper for God to do this for us because Christ died to wash away our sins.

We all fall short of glory each and every day! We live in a fallen world. Yet if we confess our sins, he who is faithful and just will forgive us our sins and cleanse us from all unrighteousness. It is our gift. All those things that get in our way and cause us anxiety, fear and doubt we get to let that go, nail it to the cross, lay it at the foot of the cross, and walk away. Sins forgiven!

James 1:12 The Voice

Happy is the person who can hold up under trials of life. At the right time, he'll know God's sweet approval and will be crowned with life. As God has promised, the crown awaits all who love Him.

Plain and simple, life can be difficult to navigate at times. I sometimes never want to leave the comfort of my own home because I feel safe and know my connection to God is secure and switched on. That is not what he wants for us. If we are going to be his light in this dark world we have to get out and be that light, interact with others, endure the trials of life. Life happens and God knows that, He wants us to be happy in every and all circumstances. By keeping his love growing in us and taking what he has shown us out in the world, we will be a blessing to our family, friends and community.

Finally, a beautiful verse from Philippians 1:9 NLT

> I pray that your love will overflow more and more, and that you will keep on growing in your knowledge and understanding.

Might these words flow over you and bless you as you continue to grow and walk with Jesus.

SEGMENT 8

~

Walking the Narrow Path

Walking the narrow path is a beautiful journey. It is a beautiful journey because we are walking with Jesus the lover of our hearts. You truly know when you are on the narrow path because you have fallen in love with Jesus. This is where we find out what true pure unconditional love is.

On my journey, I started simply reading devotionals morning and night, recited familiar prayers and scriptures. Then one day a challenge showed up in my work email inbox (of all places) and it was to read the new testament in 1 year. The only dedication it took was an open heart and 5 minutes per week day. I was already familiar with the new testament but have never read it all. As the year progressed, I started hearing and seeing the Triune God in a different light than I had previously. By the end of that year I knew Jesus in such a different, more intimate way than I ever had. The words in red were speaking to my heart so vividly. I had a better understanding of what love is and what love is not!

As we find this transforming and empowering love that is ours for eternity, it's game on! Reading the bible and getting to rekindle my relationship with Jesus was truly the 'lamp unto my feet and the light unto my path (Psalm 119:105).

As one of His very own we become a conduit. We walk His walk and take His word to the ends of the earth, while we live our lives on the narrow path. As you keep on keeping on we spread his love in each and each one of our footsteps. Our walk (strength, endurance and hope) becomes our confidence to share our testimonies. Those testimonies help others grow their spirituality as the Holy Spirit flows in and through us as we minister to others on their journey. It's easy to observe this on your own. Next time you are out and about, put on the characteristics of Jesus, notice how other people light up. Tell your story or share a story and see the blessings flourish.

As beautiful and joyful as the narrow path is, it can be a lonely path, especially if you are single or or have few like minded people in your life. When our gaze is fixed on unconditional love and we take our loneliness and other life circumstances to God, He makes our path smooth and it is easier to navigate distractions and chaos of this world in a healthy and wholistic way.

It is human to focus on the distractions we see on our horizontal but as we grow and walk more confidently on the narrow path, we stay anchored to God.

In this segment we will gain understanding of the narrow path. We will learn that you might be lonely but you are never alone. The Lord, our Father, and Jesus Christ, His Son, and the Holy Spirit walk with you. You will meet people on your journey that will pour goodness (plant seeds) into your growth, there will be people that will bring up things from your past and you will meet people that will be with you for eternity in some way, shape, or form. God places assignments in our path and opportunities in our path both are to grow our spiritual connection to the Creator of all things.

Day 1 Morning

Find a comfortable restorative pose, one hand on heart one hand on belly recognizing the breath as it flows through the body. Enjoy the silence and calmness for at least 2 minutes, paying attention to the breath, the gentle rise and fall of the chest and belly.

Silence, stillness and centering for a minimum of 2 minutes on:
I am light. I am love. I am peace.

Devotional reading:

Matthew 7:13-14 TLB

Heaven can be entered only through the narrow gate! The highway to hell is broad, and its gate is wide enough for all the multitudes who choose its easy way. But the Gateway to life is small, and the road is narrow, and only a few ever find it.

When you have entered the narrow gate and are walking the narrow path, your mind opens to living heaven on earth. The indwelling of the Holy Spirit amps up our ability to walk and live our lives in His peace and joy. Is it easy? Absolutely not! That is why the 'other' gate is broad, it's easy and anyone can get in. Surrendering (dying to our self imposed identities, temptations and handing control over to God) each and every day takes strength and endurance. The reward of the narrow path is living your life like it's heaven on earth. For me, surrendering was like handing over the keys to my car, and admitting to God that okay I kinda ran this into the ground here, how about you take the keys from here on out. It was my rock bottom day that I made that promise to God. And it took strength like I never had before and endurance to keep on keeping on, yet that endurance produced the faith in which I live today. The narrow path is the only path for me!

Journal:

What came up for you while reading this devotion? Are you on the narrow path or broad path? Where do you need God's help to stay on the narrow path?

Morning Prayer:

Let my eyes stay on Jesus and the narrow path. Amen.

Nourishment:

Enjoy a cup of lemon water to prepare your body for the day.

Movement:

Standing in Mountain Position, interlace your fingers behind your back. Roll the shoulders to the back body and tilt the chin to the ceiling. Take three cleansing breaths over the front side of the heart. This allows the tension to roll off our shoulders while opening the heart and throat chakras.

Day 1 Evening

Nourishment:

Enjoying a cup of hot lemon water to help slow down your body and mind for restoration.

Slowing the movement:

From a comfortable reclined restorative position, place both hands on the belly. Recognize the rise and fall of the breath. Relax in silence for a minimum of 2 minutes.

Silence, stillness and centering on:
I am joyful. I am blessed. I am at peace.

Devotional:

Matthew 7:13-14 The Passion

Come to God through the narrow gate, because the wide gate and broad path is the way that leads to destruction – nearly everyone chooses that crowded road! The narrow gate and the difficult way leads to eternal life – so few even find it!

Going with the flow, and sticking with the crowd is the path of least resistance. Patient endurance gives us the strength and stamina to prayerfully stay the course through the narrow gate.

Journal:

Review your day. How have you been able to create space in the body, mind and soul to allow God to keep you on the narrow path? Where did you resist and where did you patiently endure? Journal those things you are thankful for and those things for which you remain hopeful.

Additional journal prompts for overall health and wellness:
~nourishment
~movement

Pray.

Day 2 Morning

Find a comfortable restorative pose, one hand on heart one hand on belly recognizing the breath as it flows through the body. Enjoy the silence and calmness for at least 2 minutes, paying attention to the breath, the gentle rise and fall of the chest and belly.

Silence, stillness and centering for a minimum of 2 minutes on:
I am light. I am love. I am peace.

Devotional reading:

Proverbs 2:6-10 The Passion

Wisdom is a gift from a generous God, and every word he speaks is full of revelation and becomes a fountain of understanding within you.

For the Lord has a hidden storehouse of wisdom made accessible to his godly lovers.

He becomes your personal bodyguard as you follow his ways, protecting and guarding you as you choose what is right.

Then you will discover all that is just, proper, and fair, and be empowered to make the right decisions as you walk into your destiny.

When wisdom wins your heart and revelation breaks in, true pleasure enters your soul.

We all have giftings from the Holy Spirit. You may or may not know what those giftings are yet. As I became more aware of my gift of sensing angels and being more intuitive with the Holy Spirit, I became more confident in reading and understanding situations as they occurred. In some situations I "call on" or check with the angels. When you first start realizing these gifts of the Spirit, it isn't something you want to advertise. At least, I didn't. Over time I became more comfortable with sharing my gifts. At first it was mostly with my kids. The first time I let them in on this was during a summer trip to Toronto. This was much earlier on in my journey, when I was first getting to know the narrow path, and was still bumping into the guard rails (as it were) often. My daughter and I took the 'red eye' into Toronto, landing just after 5 in the morning. I have always had a fear of Toronto and the taxi drivers there. As we walked with our luggage toward the exit, I prayed. I was praying away my normal anxiety which I had about taxis in Toronto. As we were making our way towards the taxi exit, a soft voice said 'Did you need a ride?' I turned and said yes. As my daughter looked at me I could see sheer fear and panic in her eyes. I knew the look, I am a mom. She gave me that 'never accept a ride from a stranger' look. No sooner did she take my arm and whisper in my ear 'Should we be doing this?' I said, 'It's okay honey, I checked with the Angels'. She was definitely doubting me and I was new at this so it kind of had me doubting the whole process too. But as we walked into the car garage, I continued checking with the 'Angels' and the message seemed to be pure, peaceful and sincere, so we rolled with that. Of course, I wouldn't advise taking rides from complete strangers, but once you begin to understand how the Spirit moves you or how God speaks to you through people, circumstances or your 'Angels', you can be confident to take that advice and move where God is moving you. The driver turned out to be a lovely soul and also a fellow Christian. When I have had these types of encounters they usually end in the person randomly saying to me 'God bless you'. Not only do I believe in angels I believe I have three body guards that roll with me at all times: Father, Son and Holy Spirit.

> When angels visit us, we do not hear the rustle of wings, nor feel the feathery touch of the breast of a dove; but we know their presence by the love they create in our hearts.

"Unlikely Angels" - *Extraordinary Women* by Julie Clinton

Journal:

What came up for you while reading this devotion? How does God speak to your heart? What revelations or breakthroughs have you had over the past week?

Morning Prayer:

Holy Spirit you are welcome here. Amen.

Nourishment:

Enjoy a cup of lemon water to prepare your body for the day.

Movement:

Standing in Mountain Position, interlace your fingers behind your back. Roll the shoulders to the back body and tilt the chin to the ceiling. Take three cleansing breaths over the front side of the heart. This allows the tension to roll off our shoulders while opening the heart and throat chakras.

Day 2 Evening

Nourishment:

Enjoying a cup of hot lemon water to help slow down your body and mind for restoration.

Slowing the movement:

From a comfortable reclined restorative position, place both hands on the belly. Recognize the rise and fall of the breath. Relax in silence for a minimum of 2 minutes.

Silence, stillness and centering on:
I am joyful. I am blessed. I am at peace.

Devotional:

> Deuteronomy 32:1-4 NLT
>
> Listen, O heavens, and I will speak!
> Hear, O earth, the words that I say!
> Let my teaching fall on you like rain;
> let my speech settle like dew.
> Let my words fall like rain on tender grass,
> like gentle showers on young plants.
> I will proclaim the name of the Lord;
> how glorious is our God!
> He is the Rock; his deeds are perfect.
> Everything he does is just and fair.
> He is a faithful God who does no wrong;
> how just and upright he is!

This scripture is beautiful and uplifting. It helps me remember where my anchor is set and why it is set. This scripture refreshes my body, mind and soul and fills me with his goodness. As your read this scripture over a second time try and place yourself in this setting and feel God refresh your body, mind and soul.

Journal:

Review your day. How have you been able to create space in the body, mind and soul to allow God to refresh you? Where is your anchor set? Journal those things you are thankful for and things you remain hopeful of.

Additional journal prompts for overall health and wellness:
~*nourishment*
~*movement*

Pray.

Day 3 Morning

Find a comfortable restorative pose, one hand on heart one hand on belly recognizing the breath as it flows through the body. Enjoy the silence and calmness for at least 2 minutes, paying attention to the breath, the gentle rise and fall of the chest and belly.

Silence, stillness and centering for a minimum of 2 minutes on:
I am light. I am love. I am peace.

Devotional reading:

Psalm 25:4-12 The Voice

Taking wise words from the song of David:

DEMONSTRATE Your ways, O Eternal One. Teach me to understand so I can follow.

EASE me down the path of Your truth.
FEED me Your word
because You are the True God who has saved me.
I wait all day long, hoping, trusting in You.

GRACIOUS Eternal One, remember Your compassion; rekindle Your concern and love,
which have always been part of Your actions towards those who are Yours.
Do not HOLD against me the sins I committed when I was young;
instead, deal with me according to Your mercy and love.

Then Your goodness may be demonstrated in all the world, Eternal One.

IMMENSELY good and honorable is the Eternal; that's why He teaches sinners the way.
With JUSTICE, He directs the humble in all that is right,
and He shows them His way.
KIND and true are all the ways of the Eternal
to the people who keep His covenant and His words.

O LORD, the Eternal, bring glory to Your name, and forgive my sins because they are beyond number.

MAY anyone who fears the Eternal
be shown the path he should choose.

We are all in the Jesus apprenticeship program. Thanks to Jesus, our sins (which there are many) are forgiven because he died on the cross to save all sinners. David here sings about being open to the Lord and his teaching. We are reminded again that we are eased down the road with the word of God.

Journal:

What came up for you while reading this devotion? What path is God helping you choose? Where in your day can you lean into God's mercy and love to stay on the path?

Morning Prayer:

Lord let me celebrate your love so that I can lean into your guidance today. Amen.

Nourishment:

Enjoy a cup of lemon water to prepare your body for the day.

Movement:

Standing in Mountain Position, interlace your fingers behind your back. Roll the shoulders to the back body and tilt the chin to the ceiling. Take three cleansing breaths over the front side of the heart. This allows the tension to roll off our shoulders while opening the heart and throat chakras.

Day 3 Evening

Nourishment:

Enjoying a cup of hot lemon water to help slow down your body and mind for restoration.

Slowing the movement:

From a comfortable reclined restorative position, place both hands on the belly. Recognize the rise and fall of the breath. Relax in silence for a minimum of 2 minutes.

Silence, stillness and centering on:
I am joyful. I am blessed. I am at peace.

Devotional:

Matthew 6:34 The Voice

So do not worry about tomorrow. Let tomorrow worry about itself. Living faithfully is a large enough task for today.

Friends, there is a reason I like to do an examen, a personal inventory at the end of my day to reflect where I was present to God's love throughout my day and where I was least present. It establishes my roots, it sets my anchor on my Rock so that, I can realize the grace God gives me to live faithfully. When you can honestly recognize where we can grow in strength, endurance and patience we can let go of the control and loosen our grip on our worries and anxieties.

Journal:

Review your day. How have you been able to create space in the body, mind and soul to allow you to keep on the narrow path and not worry? Where can you add more endurance and patience in your daily activities? Journal those things you are thankful for and things you remain hopeful of.

Additional journal prompts for overall health and wellness:
~nourishment
~movement

Pray.

Day 4 Morning

Find a comfortable restorative pose, one hand on heart one hand on belly recognizing the breath as it flows through the body. Enjoy the silence and calmness for at least 2 minutes, paying attention to the breath, the gentle rise and fall of the chest and belly.

Silence, stillness and centering for a minimum of 2 minutes on:
I am light. I am love. I am peace.

Devotional reading:

On my journey, I have found it helpful to place my life before God each and every day.

Romans 12:1-2 The Message

So here's what I want you to do, God helping you: Take your everyday, ordinary life – your sleeping, eating, going to work, and walking around life – and place it before God as an offering. Embracing what God does for you is the best thing you can do for him. Don't become so well-adjusted to your culture that you fit into it without even thinking. Instead, fix your attention on God. You'll be changed from the inside out. Readily recognize what he wants from you, and quickly respond to it. Unlike the culture around you, always dragging you down to its level of immaturity, God brings the best out of you, develops well-formed maturity in you.

God cares about every aspect of our lives! When we embrace what God does for us – he delights in our ways. When we praise him for the answered and unanswered prayers, he rejoices. When we fix our attention to God we open up the path which 'leads us to a beautiful life, where the treasures are never ending and we can experience true joy and contentment' (Psalm 16:11).

One memorable moment on my journey was the day the words of the well known hymn: *What a Friend we have in Jesus,* came to life in my life. The things I was experiencing and the growth I was seeing in my spiritual journey were things I didn't really have anyone to talk to about. That is the day Jesus truly became my best friend. Singing this hymn would fill me with joy and cleanse me body, mind and soul. It really came to life when our missionary pastor sang it in Korean. I don't know a single word of Korean, but as he sang one verse of the song it was like my soul understood every word. One might think, well it was the piano or organ, but it was just his voice singing those words that feed my soul. I encourage you to meditate on the words of this hymn as you read through it see what stirs your heart.

Appendix G - Hymn - What a Friend we have in Jesus

I realize some people struggle revealing all to God in their prayers, petitions and journals. They think He only wants to hear how good we are. This is not true. He wants to hear it all. Plus he knows all already, so he is ready to comfort us when we do place everything at his feet and seek his goodness and direction in our lives. Allow his lovingkindness to help you grow and progress further down the narrow path.

Journal:

What came up for you while reading this devotion? What do you need to do to place every aspect of your life before God? Where in your day can you lean into God's love and mercy?

Morning Prayer:

Lord let me celebrate your love so that I can lean into your guidance today. Amen.

Nourishment:

Enjoy a cup of lemon water to prepare your body for the day.

Movement:

Standing in Mountain Position, interlace your fingers behind your back. Roll the shoulders to the back body and tilt the chin to the ceiling. Take three cleansing breaths over the front side of the heart. This allows the tension to roll off our shoulders while opening the heart and throat chakras.

Day 4 Evening

Nourishment:

Enjoying a cup of hot lemon water to help slow your body and mind down for restoration.

Slowing the movement:

From a comfortable reclined restorative position, place both hands on the belly. Recognize the rise and fall of the breath. Relax in silence for a minimum of 2 minutes.

Silence, stillness and centering on:
I am joyful. I am blessed. I am at peace.

Devotional:

Psalm 118:27+29 AMP

The Lord is God, and He has given us light (illuminating us with His grace and freedom and joy)...O give thanks to the Lord, for He is good; For His lovingkindness endures forever.

As you slow down your day and read this scripture take a refreshing breath and bask in His illumination of grace, freedom and joy.

Journal:

Review your day. How have you been able to create space in the body, mind and soul to illuminate with God's grace, freedom and joy? How can you lean into his lovingkindness that endures forever? Journal those things you are thankful for and the things for which you remain hopeful.

Additional journal prompts for overall health and wellness:
~nourishment
~movement

Pray.

Day 5 Morning

Find a comfortable restorative pose, one hand on heart one hand on belly recognizing the breath as it flows through the body. Enjoy the silence and calmness for at least 2 minutes, paying attention to the breath, the gentle rise and fall of the chest and belly.

Silence, stillness and centering for a minimum of 2 minutes on:
I am light. I am love. I am peace.

Devotional reading:

Psalm 27:4-6 The Message

I'm asking God for one thing,
Only one thing:
To live with him in his house
My whole life long.

I'll contemplate his beauty;
I'll study at his feet.

That's the only quiet, secure place
In a noisy world,
The perfect getaway,
Far from the buzz of traffic.

God holds me head and shoulders
Above all who try to pull me down.
I'm headed for his place to offer anthems
That will raise the roof!
Already I'm singing God-songs;
I'm making music to God.

Such a lovely Psalm! Sometimes I get a little too cozy at His feet, studying His word, and I forget to take his message to the streets. We are meant to serve, to be his rain worm, moving soil in his vineyard. It is wonderful to sit in restoration and study at his feet, but that is not the only thing He wants from us. We are relational creatures, we have been created to interact with others as well as spread His word to the ends of the earth. For me, this means I am not supposed to just sing his songs in my house or in my community but really sing his praises and take it to the street. As uncomfortable as it is for me to move out of my comfort zone, He encourages me to do so. When I am out in that zone He finds a way to place the people into my path that He wants me to touch with his love and light. I have been truly blessed that He has placed the most amazing people in my life for sometimes just an instant or sometimes for a lengthier assignment. As we minister to those He places in our lives (knowingly or unknowingly) we see significant growth in our own spiritual journey. We gain confidence through sharing our testimonies as we walk like Jesus, while walking the narrow path. The more we share, the more energy we create to singing his praises everywhere we go. Getting out of that comfort zone and sharing is a tall order but I know first hand we can do it!

Journal:

What came up for you while reading this devotion? What praises can you sing about today? Where can you take his message today?

Morning Prayer:

Lord let me celebrate your love so that I can lean into your guidance today. Amen.

Nourishment:

Enjoy a cup of lemon water to prepare your body for the day.

Movement:

Standing in Mountain Position, interlace your fingers behind your back. Roll the shoulders to the back body and tilt the chin to the ceiling. Take three cleansing breaths over the front side of the heart. This allows the tension to roll off our shoulders while opening the heart and throat chakras.

Day 5 Evening

Nourishment:

Enjoying a cup of hot lemon water to help slow down your body and mind for restoration.

Slowing the movement:

From a comfortable reclined restorative position, place both hands on the belly. Recognize the rise and fall of the breath. Relax in silence for a minimum of 2 minutes.

Silence, stillness and centering on:
I am joyful. I am blessed. I am at peace.

Devotional:

Be a lighthouse for others still in the dark.

Matthew 5:14-16 The Voice

And you, beloved, are the light of the world. A city built on a hilltop cannot be hidden. Similarly it would be silly to light a lamp and then hide it under a bowl. When someone lights a lamp, she puts it on a table or a desk or a chair, the the light illumines the entire house. You are like that illuminating light. Let your light shine everywhere you go, that you may illumine creation, so men and women everywhere may see your good actions, may see creation at its fullest, may see your devotion to Me, and may turn and praise Father in heaven because of it.

We are all where we are. We have all visited the dark. Let your light shine everywhere you go. It only takes a spark.

Journal:

Review your day. How have you been able to create space in the body, mind and soul to act as a lighthouse in someone else's darkness? In what ways can you be a lighthouse? Journal those things you are thankful for and those things for which you remain hopeful.

Additional journal prompts for overall health and wellness:
~nourishment
~movement

Pray.

Segment 8 was about walking the narrow path. Taking our Christ-like qualities to the street, to the people, His people. On my personal pilgrimage, as I began to walk the narrow path I started to experience heightened sensory awareness. This awareness is amplified when our chakras are aligned and we have a good energy flow within the body. It is truly a gift to be able to sense angels and actually feel the rush of the Holy Spirit flow through my body as He speaks to me. As life on my journey progressed I realized I had other sensational gifts which I am going to continue to explore and allow Christ to develop them in me. We all have gifts, I encourage you to identify and cultivate those gifts.

Maybe your gift is being a lighthouse for others. I know I have a light that shines bright in me. Those who have the gift to see the light know that I am a light bearer and have commented on my aura and my light within. I am not an expert on the topic but when I asked those who see my light they have explained that those who can see the light can see chakras, auras or the light within. Some people can sense energy, good or bad or evil. My first yoga studio was located in an old Anglican church. It was wonderful! I remember one day when an older lady walked in and she just stood there with her hands on her heart. Then she raised her hands to God and looked at me and said, 'I can feel the prayers of all the many years this was a church'. She introduced herself as the Diacan from the Anglican church in Moose Jaw. The church she was standing in was once her parish. The next summer, at the annual summer festival that brought thousands of tourists to our village a woman walked in and came up to me and wanted to let me know the energy from that church called to her as she walked down the street and she needed to come meet me. The beauty of those kinds of encounters encouraged me to lean into the gifts that God gave me. Always checking back with him to ensure I am on the path in which He is leading me. If you start to notice sensations that you don't understand bring it to God just to ensure you are in alignment. We know that Jesus was sensational to energy; one example is from the story in the Gospel of Mark 5:27-34 where he encounters the woman who was hemorrhaging for years. Jesus sensed energy leaving his body which healed this woman. 'Lots of people were pressed against Jesus at the moment, but He immediately felt her touch; He felt healing power flow out of him' (Mark 5:30 The Voice). In this example Jesus didn't touch her but she touched him. She was healed immediately. When she confesses that she was the one that touched Jesus, his response is that her faith healed her. Faith is the cornerstone on this journey. You gotta have faith!

Jesus wants us to go back to the same awe, wonder and joy that we knew when we were kids. To sensationalize and recognize the beauty of all creation. The narrow path offers that. A solid spiritual connection is vital to our lives and livelihood. When our anchor is set on the Rock of our salvation, we can establish the roots of our vertical so that nothing on the horizontal will take us down. As we become diligent at presenting our horizontal infractions to God and faithfully lay them at the foot of the cross the healing can begin to transform our body, mind and soul.

What I have found walking the narrow path is that not only can it be nurturing and joyful, it can also become lonely at times. We are relational creatures! We are wired to love and be loved. Finding like minded people can at times be difficult. When it gets lonely on the narrow path, I find it helps to get out of my comfort zone. I go find a new place or way to bring joy back to my narrow path.

This past summer I was feeling lonely, I was at the end of a 3 year relationship that I was hopeful would eventually go somewhere. But instead of it going somewhere, it was simply feeding my loneliness and my relational expectations were not being met. I found myself needing to take a personal inventory and what I realized was a reset was needed because what I thought might be my forever, was tempting me off the narrow path.

I had been asking God daily for signs and his direction about this relationship. I knew I needed to get myself focused. The phrase in 1 Corinthians 13 came to mind and what I realized is love doesn't want what love doesn't have. If this person I loved was not ready to move forward and if he could not love me as a partner should then he was not mine and very simply love does not want what love does not have! Me continuing to want and wait was tempting me to place this person as an idol in my life, which I was not wanting to do. Sometimes we don't even realize that we are placing other things or people above God thus, creating an idol. Keeping the love of God in that sacred space and trusting in Him with all your heart, mind, soul and strength even when temptations or regular life circumstances show up on the horizontal.

Finding that spot where God speaks to you is important. God speaks to me in nature and sometimes I just need to get out in the middle of a forest, on a rock in the middle of a canola field, standing at the edge of a flax field watching the blooms as if they are waves in the ocean or at the top of a hill so that I can find the peace where he speaks to my heart. In the situation from this past summer, I did just that, I prayed for answers, I assured God I only wanted to be on the narrow path going only where he wants me to go. And in a canola field standing on a rock, I felt the presence of God assuring me that the narrow path *can* be lonely and we *are* relational creatures and what I was feeling was stuff from my past that needed to be addressed. Things come up so that they can come out and help us to mature and grow in Christ and keep us on our way down the narrow path.

Walking the narrow path also gives you opportunities to work on healthy boundaries for those relationships that do not fuel your soul with joy. Sometimes we need to run fast from those things or those people that bring toxins or negative energy into our lives. There is no reason to tolerate inappropriate behaviours. The best alternative is to speak the truth as lovingly as possible to the person, set healthy boundaries, and respectfully disengage from that person if they push the boundaries you have placed. I find it useful to set a healthy boundary then pray for that person. I pray the Placing the Cross Prayer which can be found in Appendix B. You should never fear placing the cross between yourself and anyone. The cross breaks unhealthy ties and unholy bonds. This organically weeds people out of your life God's way.

All things happen for a reason and in whatever season. God has made everything beautiful for its time and everything God does endures forever. Nothing can be added; nothing taken away; we can just stand in awe (adapted from Ecclesiastes 3). The best thing I have learned (and it has taken numerous lessons over and over) is not to worry. Be content on the narrow path.

Have the endurance, the strength — the body, mind and soul — to persevere all the trials in life. Finding healthy ways to deal with the infractions that happen on the horizontal will keep you anchor attached to the Rock. Knowing that when we are weak, He is strong. As we place our life and our circumstances before Him and trust in Him, we strengthen our vertical. The scripture that comes to mind for me when I need to strengthen my vertical:

Ephesians 3:17-19 The Amplified Bible

...so that Christ may dwell in your hearts through your faith. And may you, having been (deeply) rooted and (securely) grounded in love, be fully capable of comprehending with all the saints (God's people) the width and length and height and depth of His love (fully experiencing that amazing, endless love); and (that you may come) to know (practically, through personal experience) the love of Christ which far surpasses (mere) knowledge (without experience), that you may be filled up (throughout your being) to all the fullness of God (so that you may have the richest experience of God's presence in your lives, completely filled and flooded with God himself).

As we experience the richness and fullness of God, we begin to recognize our gifts and then cultivate our gifts. I know that through my experiences God has called me to be his servant and help others. I know, without a doubt, that Jesus asked me to tell my story. I've been prompted on so many speaking occasions by the Spirit to share, and even thought often what I shared was not in my prepared script, a new script would speak through me. Each time this has happened, I have had at least one (sometimes many) come up after saying 'that is exactly what I needed to hear today'.

He asked me to write this book and to help all those he sends me – to willingly take on the assignments he has given me. I've tried to turn away from some assignments, but our God has a sense of humour and the assignment continues to show up until He says we are done.

Sometimes these assignments are meant to strengthen others while there are times assignments are for our own growth, our next level of enlightenment. Sometimes the assignments can bring about difficult circumstances. No matter the circumstance, no matter the hardships, I find it beneficial to say over and over: I can do all things through Christ who strengthens me! I chant it repeatedly some days when the struggle feels real. I am confident he is strengthening me.

We each have a divine calling and this scripture helps remember my calling:

Ephesians 4:2-4 The Passion

With tender humility and quiet patience, always demonstrate gentleness and generous love towards one another, especially toward those who may try your patience. Be faithful to guard the sweet harmony of the Holy Spirit among you in the bonds of peace, being one body and one spirit, as you were called into the same glorious hope of divine destiny.

Oh my heavens I love that scripture! So poetic and graceful! When we can focus on that divine destination, keeping our eyes on Jesus we will walk poetically and gracefully.

Through my God assignments on my spiritual walk, I discovered I am meant to pray and be a conduit of his love and the light as He leads me on my journey. I have come to realize that his gifts are more plentiful when I relax and lean into Him. As we grow our spiritual gifts it is helpful to remember that we only know what we know through our unique experiences in life. What we know needs to be shared, just as He has placed significant people or events in our life to guide us, He has placed people in our paths for us to inspire. If we share our story and can save one person from falling down, we have done what Jesus has asked.

God wants us to choose the narrow path and get away from the buzz and traffic. Yet, he challenges us to get out and take His gospel to the ends of the earth while sticking to His path. Yes, a delicate line to tap dance. However, I assert that as we steady our anchor to the Rock of our salvation, tap dancing that delicate line becomes the most enjoyable time of your life!

It will be a journey of listening and learning and as we are reminded in Romans 10:17 (The Message) "Before you can trust, you have to listen. But unless Christ's Word is preached, there's nothing to listen to." I assert that we are being asked to take His word, His goodness, to walk His walk and to talk up the goodness, because the journey leads to one ultimate destination so while we are on that journey might as well talk up Jesus! Very true not everyone will want to hear or want to believe. I believe that each of us has the seed of love and the breath of the Holy Spirit within us all. We can be accepting or reluctant. To believe is a choice to surrender is the action of our choice. The more we let Him in the more healing we can bring to ourselves and others.

Inspirational Devotional:

Psalm 103:3-5, 8-9 and 11-12 The Passion

You've kissed my heart with forgiveness, in spite of all
I've done.
You've healed me inside and out from every disease.
You've rescued me from hell and saved my life.
You've crowned me with love and mercy.
You satisfy my every desire with good things.
You've supercharged my life so that I soar again like a
flying eagle in the sky!

Lord, you're so kind and tenderhearted to those who
don't deserve it and so patient with people who fail you!
Your love is like a flooding river overflowing its banks
with kindness.
You don't look at us only to find faults, just so that you
can hold a grudge against us.

Higher than the highest heavens – that's how high
your tender mercy extends!
Greater than the grandeur of heaven above is the
greatness of your loyal love, towering over all who fear
you and bow down before you!

Farther than from a sunrise to a sunset – that's how far
you've removed our guilt from us.

This entire Psalm is fascinating, for today let's just let these words stir our hearts, knowing God's lovingkindness and mercy are with us and his forgiveness is as wide as East is to West. Can we be as forgiving and loving as we are loved?

May these words from Philippians 4:5-9 (NIV) bless your journey and guide you to an intimate relationship with the Triune God.

> Let your gentleness be evident to all. The Lord is near. Do not be anxious about anything, but in every situation, by prayer and petition, with thanksgiving, present your request to God. And the peace of God, which transcends all understand, will guard your hearts and your minds in Christ Jesus.

Conclusion

I want to personally thank you for taking time to join in this 40 day journey with me. Even if it took you more than the suggested 40 days, know that you are on the right path. It is truly a walk of grace. I prayerfully hope that the Holy Spirit met you exactly where you are at in your own personal journey.

I only know what I know and I hope what I have shared has helped you in some way find direction in your current struggles or your own spiritual journey. I have found that the 40 day treatments have worked dynamically in my life. Both to find spiritual direction for myself or pray for the needs of others.

I can tell you only this, the indwelling of the Holy Spirit has healed me from so much *dis-ease* and ailments in my body. It has helped me find strength to forgive myself and others. It has helped me find healthy ways to deal with the trauma I have suffered from abuse.

By allowing the Holy Spirit to be my anchor I can deal with the waves and the winds. By inviting Jesus into my heart and my life, I have secured my vertical. All that takes place on the horizontal will no longer take me down. Sure it might distract me(I am human after all!) but if I have Jesus in my heart, my vertical remains strong.

Being disciplined spiritually allows for healthy relationships with every aspect of your life. It becomes a new regular routine for healthy living. It allows you to re-invest in life fully. The inside-out rule to healing is essentially found by embracing the one thing that Jesus asks us to do – LOVE. To model His ways, to walk with Him. When we abide in Him and Him in us there is no law opposed to those things. When we are circulating and percolating in the realm, the frequency, and the vibration of love, we are doing what we have been asked to do. Think about the love and joy and peace you experience in that realm. To me, it is like heaven on earth! We are human and if we are going to be the rain worm in the Lord's vineyard, we are going to ultimately have to interact with other humans. For me that was the hard part. The new me was not always graceful getting out and intermingling with humans. He doesn't just want us to sit and worship Him, heavens no, He wants us to get our boots dusty and walk with Him.

I have gained valuable knowledge on this journey and accept that all is grace. I have grace with myself to know that I am human, I will not be my best self one hundred percent of the time, nor will those I encounter on the horizontal be their best either. When we have our anchor to God our vertical aligned with him, when things start to happen on the horizontal I encourage you to bring it back to your spiritual connection, as quickly as it happens. Things like fear, doubts, anxiety and insecurities will try and take us down on the horizontal, as will guilt and shame. Infractions to the vertical from the horizontal will intersect us whether by our own doings or by the actions of others. Having grace in our relationships with others while allowing God to be our sure and steady anchor we can offer grace and forgiveness to others as God forgives us too for our infractions on ourselves and others. A helpful reminder for me which I come back to often is that God forgives us as far from the east as it is to the west, he forgives our sins. He asks us to simply not sin again. Sins forgiven. Sure, you will sin again. We were born both saint and sinner, we live in a fallen world. But it is us who hold ourselves down. God doesn't. He is waiting to hear from us and place everything at his feet, or to nail it to the cross. To let it go and just do the things he asked us to do. I have found that by doing a daily office, by constantly (or as constant as I can) be in contact with Him the better I am at recognizing the winds or the waves on the horizontal. My reminder to stand firm. I find too that taking the personal inventory and journaling about my day helps me uncover areas that I still need to work on. It is a learning journey. The more we learn about ourselves, who we are and where we came from and who we are in Christ will help us cultivate our gifts, the fruits of the Spirit.

I am hopeful this book has helped you find a way to enjoy being a beloved child of God. As I am reminded from my favourite Lenten devotional Sacred Silence by Phyllis Zagano:

> "Our natural histories are sacred and special, each of us has within us the spark of God, the Light that gives light to our souls. That life is a participation in the life of God, and when we recognize that in ourselves we can begin at the least to recognize it in others, especially in Jesus. If we are able to see each person before us as part of Christ's participation in the world, we will – I think – begin to understand what Jesus is talking about"

The further we lean into our Christ-like qualities, taking time to mature them and grow our own spiritual discipline, the more patient and accepting we become of the people and the circumstances we face. As we grow and accept more of the 'spark of God, the Light that gives light to our souls' the more relaxed and comfortable this life gets.

One of my favorite scriptures that brings light to my path and keeps me centred is Psalm 16:11 (The Voice), A prayer of David: 'Instead he directs me on a path that leads to a beautiful life, as I walk with him the pleasures are never ending and I know true joy and contentment.' A beautiful life waits in His Light. You, a willing participant, can live in that joy and contentment too!

There will be many of you who will put this book up on the shelf, and that is fine. However for those of you whose hearts were stirred in some way, I encourage you to take that to the streets. Just know that your story and your experience might help someone else. I have always said that if I have touched just one heart, I have done what Jesus has asked me to do.

Our spiritual connection to the love of God truly is a mystery and we need to be okay and content with that, with the not knowing, not being in control of the outcome. Accept the now and wait to see where He is leading you next. We are reminded of this in the following scripture: Matthew 16:24 (NKJV) Jesus said to His disciples. "If anyone desires to come after Me, let him deny himself, and take up his cross, and follow Me."

What Jesus wants is for us to live free, to walk His walk, surrender (let go of) the things that bring us into the storms of this world. He died for us. He died for the forgiveness of all our sins. He just wants us to take those things of which we need to let go and nail them to the cross. Repentance equals salvation. He wants us to unburden ourselves with this life and live the life He wants us to live. And that, my dear friend, is living a life of love!

Jeremiah 6:16 (NIV) encourages us to 'Stand at the crossroads and look; ask for the ancient paths, ask where the good way is, and walk in it.' To walk the ancient paths, to walk where the good way is, is to take our Christ-like qualities and be open to where the Spirit guides us. To walk the 'good way' is to have a spiritual discipline that keeps the vertical aligned to the Source of light then to take that light and display it in each step we take. It is to be a blessing and a source of encouragement to others by sharing our unique stories. Those stories may be the hope and strength that others need on their own journey.

My strength is in the Triune God and I know that He is in me and I am in Him. I do my very best to live my life in the light of His love allowing myself to be led by the Spirit. To live my life as Psalm 84:5 outlines: 'Blessed are those whose strength is in you, whose hearts are set on pilgrimage.' To walk in the ways of God, we have to move our feet!

My hope is that what I shared from my personal pilgrimage will help you establish a spiritual discipline that will bring you closer to God, while healing you from the inside out. And as you heal from the inside out, I pray that leads you closer to having a healthy relationship to every single situation or circumstance you face along your own pilgrimage.

Ephesians 3:17-19 The Passion

Then, by constantly using your faith, the life of Christ will be released deep inside you, and the resting place of his love will become the very source and root of your life. Then you will be empowered to discover what every holy one experiences - the great magnitude of the astonishing love of Christ in all its dimensions. How deeply intimate and far-reaching is his love! How enduring and inclusive it is! Endless love beyond measurement that transcends our understanding - this extravagant love pours into you until you are filled to overflowing with the fullness of God!

His love is empowering, and my spiritual discipline did not just give me the balance I so needed in my life, it established my personal relationship with Jesus. It took me to the next level of knowing what love is! The grace of God has empowered me to boldly be who I am and share His wonderful light and love.

Hold tight to the fact that all is grace, just keep placing one foot in front of the other as you walk the narrow path. I do love hearing how these words may have touched your heart personally and I invite you to reach out to me on one of my social media platforms. If you would like to go deeper or if you need help developing your own spiritual discipline routine, visit anitastettner.com, I do take on a limited number of students and would love to work with you personally if the Spirit guides your path to me.

May God's peace rule your heart!

About the Author

Anita Stettner lives a life that cultivates kindness, peace and love in every footstep she takes. Passionate about her work as a spiritual yogi, coach and mentor where she has helped those led to her (by the Spirit) who have struggled with trauma, addictions and living a balanced life in this fallen world. As a prayer warrior she loves the opportunity to make a difference in the lives of others one prayer at a time.

Anita is a mother of two living a Spirit-led life in small town Saskatchewan. After years of chasing a self-directed path, she has now found the peaceful path that leads to a beautiful life. As she walks this path the pleasures are never-ending and she now knows true joy and contentment. Lover of nature, she has found beauty in all that surrounds her, chasing sunsets, sunrises, the moon and the outdoors. She has found what love is! That love has provided a peace that transcends all understanding.

Struggling with her own chaotic life, her journey led her to The Bible, Jesus, yoga and an overall healthy balanced lifestyle. Once she surrendered the self-directed path and jumped on the Spirit-led path, her life began to flourish then blossom into true freedom.

This Spirit-led life gave her the confidence to make courageous changes in her life so that her vertical would be aligned with and anchored to the lover of her soul and the Creator of all things.

Her direct experience of living under a cloak of darkness, living in fear and being stuck in abusive relationships kept her circulating in a revolving door of unhealthy patterns. Not being able to heal from sexual trauma which occurred at an early age was a barnacle to her freedom. As healthy patterns started to transform her life the past trauma has been healed from the inside out. This transformed state which used to be shame, guilt, fear and doubt is now the stage to give others a voice and the courage to heal as well. Her journey to this Divine connection is truly the platform where she courageously and obediently serves God and works passionately to help others find their freedom too.

Appendix

A - The Lord's Prayer

Meditate on each line after reading it slowly:

Our Father, Who Art in Heaven
Hallowed be Thy Name
Thy Kingdom come
Thy Will be done
On earth
As in Heaven
Give us this day
Our daily bread
Forgive us our trespasses
As we forgive those who trespass against us
Lead us not into temptation
But deliver us from evil
For thine is the Kingdom, the Power and the Glory
Now and ever and unto ages of ages. Amen
(Matthew 6:9-13)

The Lord's Prayer is widely prayed, I encourage you not just to pray that regularly, I encourage you to take it apart and really get to know it and appreciate it. It wasn't until about 7 years ago that I really dug deep into the Lord's Prayer. I was finishing off my masters project for my Holy Yoga Masters Program when the Holy Spirit was prompting me to dig deeper. That in itself is a lovely story that I will share someday, but for now just know that the goodness of God brought me to the resource to dig deeper and opened up sometime into my schedule so that, I could find time to go deeper. And with that event of going deeper I had the opportunity to bring a message forward that would encourage others. What a blessing!

There are many authors that have taken apart the Lord's Prayer. My first exposure was Luther's Small Catechism. I then was introduced to Emmet Fox version which sparked me on my spiritual discipline journey. Following the Pamona of my paternal grandmother, I picked up a copy of the Our Father by Princess Ileana of Romania, Mother Alexandra. I have found this version an easy weekly meditation where each day you examine twice a day for seven days a different stanza of the prayer.

B - Placing the Cross Prayer

The following prayer I like to call the 'placing the cross' prayer. This has personally helped me in my dating life and meeting new people life. It has also been helpful prayer when I am dealing with difficult people (or porcupines) in my life.

I place the cross of my Lord and Saviour Jesus Christ between (insert the name) and I.
By the cross I break all unhealthy ties
and every unhealthy bond with them.
Allowing only, the love of God,
the Spirit of God
and the Kingdom of God between us.
In Jesus mighty name and by His authority, Amen.

We should never be afraid to place the cross between us and whomever. Trust in the Lord. I assert that once you allow him to make the decisions of who and what should be in your life the narrow path has less speed bumps.

C - Praying for Children

I believe it is important to pray over those people we love such as our children, those who are actual children and those children God has placed in our care. Might you find these words helpful to pray over your children:

Lord, I pray that you cover my children. Give them the helmet of salvation to protect their minds against messages competing for their attention. Guard their hearts Lord from anger, depression, anxiety, loneliness or anything that would make them feel unworthy of love. No weapon formed against them shall prosper. In Jesus name, Amen.

(adapted from Isaiah 54:17)

D - Praying for Friend or Family Member

When a friend or family member is confused and perhaps not certain of the right path, I will continue to encourage that person, be lovingkindness in their life plus I will pray a simple prayer for them:

Lord I pray that (insert the name) find (his/her/their) true North, I ask that you kindly break chains and obstacles from their past that may be holding them hostage from your peace and love. I pray that you guide them from the path of pain toward the path of your salvation and endless love. In Jesus name, Amen.

When you are having differences with someone or needing to remove yourself from overfunctioning in the lives of those we love this prayer might help:

Lord I ask you to bless (insert name), might (he/she/they) see my loyalty and my lovingkindness. Lord I create a scared space of love between (insert name) and I with a bridge of love so that I might be only where You need me to be in this (situation/relationship). In Jesus name I pray, Amen.

Sometimes people are placed in our lives by God, just for us to be a conduit of His love. If you are unsure, ask for a sign of encouragement. Rather than resisting the assignment I believe we should ask the Holy

Spirit to guide us through. As this conduit of God's love we are asked to be love fully expressed providing unconditional love for those He has placed in our care or asked us to love. This can be a difficult assignment and the assignment might be for the benefit of the other person, ourselves or perhaps both. Here is a prayer I have found helpful:

Since the day the Lord gave me his good news about you (insert name), I have not stopped praying for you or loving you. I pray this prayer of knowledge and insight that can only come from the Lord.

Father, may (insert name) clearly know your will and achieve the height and depth of spiritual wisdom and understanding. Amen.

(adapted from Colossians 1:9)

E - Selection of Morning Prayers

Building prayer time into your schedule is a cornerstone of a spiritual disciple practise. If you have trouble with praying, the talking to God thing I completely understand, that takes time to develop. I have provided examples for you to try based on my experience and the experience of those I have helped on their journey.

Simple morning prayer:

Your divine power has given me all things that pertain to life and godliness. Provide me your wisdom which is pure, peaceful and sincere to gently guide my emotions this day. Amen.

Simple morning prayer:

May I walk calmly, gracefully spreading love and joy today. Amen.

Morning prayer:

I arise today through the strength of heaven
Light of sun – radiance of moon,
swiftness of wind,
stability of earth,
firmness of rock.

I arise today through God's strength to pilot me
God's word to speak for me,
God's hand to guard me,
God's way to guide me.

I pray for God's protection over me
against evil and every cruel merciless power that may oppose
my body, mind and soul. I pray the same protection over
all those I love. Amen.

Morning Prayer:

Lord allow me to let go and wait patiently on you. Keep my vertical attached to you – you are my anchor Lord. Lord give me eyes to see, ears to hear and a heart open to love and be loved. Help me rest in your goodness. Keep me positive, keep me prayerful, keep my hope attached to you. Help me cultivate the beautiful soul within me, allowing me to let the best of me shine for all those you have placed in my life. Help me listen more, talk less watching that my words fill others with joy and peace which I bring from you dear Lord.

Morning Prayer:

Spare me Lord from temptation this day. Teach me to guard my tongue from useless words. Help me to always ask: is this of good report? Am I saying or doing Kingdom work? Lord give me clear eyes and judgement that throughout this day I make good choices and healthy choices. Where there is darkness, let me see light; in the midst of chaos let me find the core of stillness. Let no fear enter my soul, but teach me bravely to face problems and conflict. Let me never forget Your word leads and guides me to where I am going and who I need to be. Help me be your loving kindness and bring your light everywhere I step today. Amen.

Morning Prayer - adapted from Micah 6:8 Expanded Bible

Lord help me this day to act justly. To love mercy and display lovingkindness to others and might I walk humbly with you. In Jesus name, Amen.

Morning Resolve – This lovely devotional was passed to me via text from a dear friend of mine. I often incorporate it into my morning prayers.

I will try this day to live simple, sincere and serene life, repelling promptly every thought of discontent, anxiety discouragement, impurity and self seeking, cultivating cheerfulness, joyfulness charity and habit of holy silence; exercising economy in expenditure, generosity in giving, carefulness in conversation, diligence in appointed service, fidelity to every trust and a child like faith in God. In particular I will try to be faithful in those habits of prayer, work, study, physical exercise, eating and sleeping, which I believe the Holy Spirit has shown me to be right. And, as I cannot in my own strength do this, nor even with hope of success attempt it, I look to thee, O Lord God my Father in Jesus my Savior and ask for the gift of the Holy Spirit. Amen.

F - Selection of Evening Prayers

A well disciplined evening routine has been helpful for me to centre myself before bed and get a good night sleep. Evening prayers can be very short and simple or longer and more detailed. The Lord's prayer is something that is perfect for the end of the day as well as the morning. I have included a few that has certainly helped my prayer life as well as those whom I have mentored or coached:

The Lord's Prayer
Our Father who art in heaven,
Hallowed be thy name,
Thy kingdom come,
Thy will be done,
On earth as it is in heaven.
Give us this day our daily bread;
And forgive us our trespasses
As we forgive those
Who trespass against us;
And lead us not into temptation,
But deliver us from evil.
For thine is the kingdom
And the power and the glory
Forever and ever. Amen.

Matthew 6:9-13 (Lutheran version)

Evening prayer:

Almighty God, my heavenly Father, I have sinned against you, through my own fault, in thought, and word, and deed, in what I have done and what I have left undone. For the sake of your Son our Lord Jesus Christ, forgive me all my offenses, and grant that I may serve you in the newness of life, to the glory of Your name. Amen

(Book of Common Prayer)

Evening prayer:

May the Lord Almighty grant me and those I love a peaceful night and a perfect end.

(Book of Common Prayer)

As a Lutheran I will also confess my faith in the words The Apostles' Creed. Prayers are personal, you get to choose what is right for your spiritual practice and what best stirs your heart.

G - Hymn - What a Friend we have in Jesus

1. What a friend we have in Jesus,
   all our sins and griefs to bear;
   what a privilege to carry
   everything to God in prayer.
   Oh what peace we often forfeit,
   oh what needless pain we bear,
   all because we do not carry
   everything to God in prayer.

2. Have we trials and temptations?
   Is there trouble anywhere?
   We should never be discouraged:
   take it to the Lord in prayer.
   Can we find a friend so faithful,
   who will all our sorrows share?
   Jesus knows our every weakness:
   take it to the Lord in prayer.

3. Are we weak and heavyladen,
   cumbered with a load of care?
   Precious Saviour, still our refuge:
   take it to the Lord in prayer.
   Do thy friends despise, forsake thee?
   Take it to the Lord in prayer;
   in his arms he'll take and shield thee;
   thou wilt find a solace there.

H - Helpful quotes and scriptures

My own practise includes praying scriptures or quotes that resonates with where I am at on my personal journey. Here are a few that are dear to me:

"Blessed is he who expects nothing for he shall enjoy everything." Francis of Assisi

Hebrews 4:12 NIV
The word of God is alive and active. Sharper than any double edge sword, it penetrates even to dividing soul and spirit, joints and marrow, it judges the thoughts and attitude of the heart.

Psalm 19:7-11 NIV
The law of the Lord is perfect, refreshing the soul. The statutes of the Lord are trustworthy, making wise the simple. The precepts of the Lord are right, giving joy to the heart. The commands of the Lord are radiant, giving light to the eyes. The fear of the Lord is pure, enduring forever. The decrees of the Lord are firm, and all of them are righteous. They are more precious than gold, than much pure gold, they are sweeter than honey, than honey from the honeycomb. By them your servant is warned, in keeping them there is great reward.

Romans 12:9 The Passion
Let the inner movement of your heart always be to love one another.

Ephesians 4: 30-32 The Passion
The Holy Spirit of God has sealed you in Jesus Christ until you experience your full salvation. So never grieve the Spirit of God or take for granted his holy influence in your life. Lay aside bitter words, temper tantrums, revenge, profanity, and insults. But instead be kind and affection toward one another. Has God graciously forgiven you? Then graciously forgive one another in the depths of Christ's love.

Romans 14:19 NASB
We pursue the things which make peace and the building up of one another.

1 Thessalonians 5:14-15 The Passion
Be skilled at gently encouraging those who feel themselves inadequate. Be faithful to stand your ground. Help the weak stand again. Be quick to demonstrate patience with everyone. Resist revenge, and make sure that no one pays back evil in place of evil but always pursue doing what is beautiful to one another and to all the unbelievers.

Psalm 27:4-6 TLB

The one thing I want from God, the thing I seek most of all, is the privilege of meditating in his Temple, living in his presence every day of my life, delighting in his incomparable perfections and glory. There I'll be when troubles come. He will hide me. He will set me on a high rock out of reach of all my enemies. Then I will bring him sacrifices and sign his praises with much joy.

I - Self Soul Care Meditation

Restoration is creating a space to reflect, redirect and restore ourselves. Restoration practices allows a gentle way of honoring the body, mind, soul and strength of our being.

Silence, stillness and centering exercise for your restorative practice is to pick a song that moves your heart, that brings tears to your eyes even if you do not know why exactly. This might be a hymn, a country song or a popular top 40 hit. This is your personal practice, best to find what works for you. Some people like words, while others are moved by instrumental music. Perhaps you love the sound of the ocean or other nature sounds. Find what calms you and spend 2 minutes or more meditating.

Meditation pose: Find a comfortable restorative pose, one hand on heart one hand on belly recognizing the rise and fall of the heart.

Journal reflections:

Take time to reflect on the song you meditated to this morning. Discuss why you chose it. Discuss what came up (if anything) during the mediation.

Allow yourself to journal what came up for you over the past few days or week. Are there areas of your spiritual practice that need redirecting? What practices were uncomfortable for you and why? What was easy for you and why?

Check in with: body, mind, soul and strength. Be honest!

Pray.

J - Centering Meditation

Restoration is about creating a space to reflect, redirect and restore ourselves. Restoration practices allow a gentle way of honoring the body, mind, soul and strength of our being.

Silence, stillness and centering exercise for reflecting on ways Jesus would go off to a solitary place to be still and silent in the presence of God. Peter Scazzero explains:

"As a result, he (Jesus) is able to do the right thing, at the right time, and with the right heart. He resists the pressure of other people's expectations and leaves... For us, this same choice – to turn away from internal and external noise in order to be with God – is work, difficult work. Externally, we face the unrelenting pressure of our culture. Internally, our minds are in constant and frenzied motion. Yet as we learn to live from a wellspring of silence and stillness, we begin to experience an unimaginable richness."

Scazzero goes on to summarize the benefits of silence: "We shift away from the artificiality of the surrounding culture toward the beauty of beholding God.

We grow in our ability to wait and see what unfolds, more trusting of the love of God.

We realize how foolish our ideas are of how the world works or should work, letting go more easily of judgments, anger, and greed.

We become more compassionate.

We influence others for good out of the changes God is doing in and through us."

As we grow in our ability to enter into silence and stillness, we not only benefit ourselves but others who are in our lives.

Meditation pose: Find a comfortable restorative pose, one hand on heart one hand on belly recognizing the rise and fall of the heart.

Journal reflections:

Take time to reflect on the devotion this morning. Discuss what came up (if anything) during this reflection. What benefits are you already recognizing in the silence and stillness you have incorporated over the past two weeks?

Allow yourself to journal what came up for you over the past few days or week. Are there areas of your practice that need redirecting? What practices were uncomfortable for you and why? What was easy for you and why?

Check in with: body, mind, soul and strength. Be honest!

Pray.

K - Camino Divina

Walking the divine way is a walking meditation that allows you to combine your yogic breathing and prayer or scripture. It is an intentional prayer walk that uses centering prayer skills which enables us to open the ears of the heart so that we can hear the voice of the Divine. It is a walk and talk with our creator. It allows us to be open to hear the spirit as well as appreciate the beauty that surrounds us. Developing skills to understand how the divine speaks to your soul.

I have developed a Camino Divina event that I host for individuals or groups. On this walking meditation I take event participants to a top of a hill that has a majestic prairie view. We first descend down the hill and enjoy the view, becoming present with all God's creation while being contemplative about the joy His creation brings us. As we descend we will centre ourselves and become mindfully aware of our intentions and prayers for the journey back up the hill. As we ascend up the hill we will use our breathing to acknowledge the beauty of all His creation and while sending our prayers and intentions towards Heaven.

For those physically fit and able to jog it is an invigorating workout. And for those who just want to enjoy the peaceful sights and sounds it is incredibly soulful.

I have also hosted lake walks and forest walks which provide the similar sensations and connections to the Divine. You can treat your everyday walk as a camino divina. Let the Lord walk with you.

Visit anitastettner.com to book a Camino Divina group event.

L - Forest Bathing Meditation

The experience of forest bathing truly allows you to open up all of your senses. There is a Heritage Site Tree Farm north of the Village I live in. It is a unique spectacular forest in the middle of the bald prairies. I was exploring it one day and found the most perfect clearing in the middle of the forest that then became my forest yoga studio.

Forest bathing is a wonderful healing and soul care opportunity, all the senses come to life as we flow through some gentle yoga poses combined with both lectio divina and visio divina meditations. Infusing cedarwood with a topical body lotion or oil and massaging the insoles of the feet will likely heighten your sensations. The participants also have the opportunity to journal about their sensational discoveries.

Being out in nature and around trees is absolute soul care. You can build your own practise maybe even in your own backyard.

Visit anitastettner.com to book a Forest Bathing Meditation group event.

M - Water Meditation

Water is a wonderful aid for meditation. Relaxing in a bath and taking soul care time is good for the entire body, mind and soul.

Finding a playlist that is soothing and comforting to your alone time.

Adding Epsom salts with essential oils such as: frankincense and eucalyptus.

Adding gemstones to the bath: selenite, rose quartz, blue calcite, lapis lazuli, amethyst, green calcite, orange calcite, yellow calcite and red calcite to represent each of the chakra gemstones.

Meditation scripture examples:

A.) It's in Christ that we find out who we are and what we are living for. Long before we first heard of Christ and got our hopes up, he had his eye on us, had designs on us for glorious living, part of the overall purpose he is working out in everything and everyone.

Ephesians 1:11-12 MSG

B.) Love the Lord your God with all your heart and with all your soul and with all your mind and with all your strength…Love your neighbor as yourself. There is no commandment greater than these."

Mark 12:30-31 NIV

C.) A time to scatter stones, a time to pile them up; a time for a warm embrace, a time for keeping your distance;

Ecclesiastes 3:5

Or finding a scripture that speaks to you and your situation in life.

Read the scripture and spend time meditating on how this scripture speaks to you today.

Pray the serenity prayer:

God grant me the serenity to accept the things I cannot change; courage to change the things I can; and wisdom to know the difference. Living one day at a time; enjoying one moment at a time; accepting hardships as the pathway to peace; taking, as He did, this sinful world as it is, not as I would have it; trusting that He will make all things right if I surrender to His Will; that I may be reasonably happy in this life and supremely happy with Him forever in the next. Amen.

Relax and enjoy your soul care time!

N - Gemstone Meditations

Different gemstones offer different healing properties. What resonates with one person may not resonate the same with another. It is a personal practice and you will know when the practise is right for you. It is about being open and allowing your body, mind and soul guide you. I can only suggest what I know worked for me. My experience has led me to accept the healing vibrations of the different gemstones to heal the dis-ease within my body. Utilizing gemstones has been a powerful healing tool for many of the people I have worked with.

Heart Centered Meditation - this meditation helps cultivate love of self, love of others and acceptance of Divine love. Helps heal a broken heart.

Gemstones - Rose quartz on the chest and chrysoprase in the hands
Aromatherapy - Rose
Yoga pose - Supported reclined butterfly - which is laying with soles of the feet together, back is supported with a pillow allowing the heart to be elevated slightly higher than shoulders yet comfortable to feel relaxed. Meditating to instrumental music or silence for 15-20 mins

Speak the Truth in Love Meditation - this meditation provides wisdom which allows us to speak the truth in love to ourselves and to others.

Gemstones - Blue calcite, blue lace agate or celestite placed comfortably between heart and throat. Rhodonite in one hand and celestite in the other.

Aromatherapy - California White Sage

Yoga pose - Supported reclined starfish - which is laying with feet shoulder width apart, back is supported with a pillow allowing the heart to be elevated slightly higher than shoulders yet comfortable to feel relaxed, head hanging over the pillow allowing the chin to be up so that there is a comfortable stretch between breastplate and chin.

Meditating to instrumental music or silence for 15-20 mins

Calming and Centering Meditation - this meditation helps cultivate calming and awareness. Calms the overactive mind bringing thoughts captive to the heart space. Helps addictions and stress.

Gemstones - Rose quartz on the chest and lepidolite in the hands

Aromatherapy - lavender

Yoga pose - Supported reclined butterfly - which is laying with soles of the feet together, back is supported with a pillow allowing the heart to be elevated slightly higher than shoulders yet comfortable to feel relaxed. Meditating to instrumental music or silence for 15-20 mins

O - Seasonal Chakra Balancing - Sun Salutation Challenge

Welcome the Spring and Fall equinox and the Summer and Winter solstice by doing the 108 sun salutation challenge.

The meaning behind the number 108 is incredibly vast and varied. It is rooted in tradition, religion and mind blowing mathematics. Most relevant is that the diameter of the sun is 108 times the diameter of the Earth.

The challenge is an amazing way to invigorate our bodies and to stretch and test our limits. With every exhale we leave behind self doubt and anxiety, with every inhale we bring in peace and love from our Creator.

This invigorating practice works to cleanse our bodies and minds and strengthens us physically and mentally allowing clarity and peace of mind.

By doing this practice we offer our gratitude to our Creator for all the gifts that surround us that we normally take for granted. This is a time to offer praise and thanksgiving for Him who has abundantly provided these amazing seasonal changes.

The most amazing thing for me each time I have done this challenge. I enter into it similar to a labyrinth where I intentionally want to hear from the Lord about areas of my life where I need to ensure I am aligned with his plans for me. Each time I start my playlist I hit shuffle and it is like the Lord finds the perfect song for the perfect moment throughout the challenge.

Take time to journal after the challenge.

P - Chakra Prayer Mediation

Aromatherapy – Frankincense

Music – choice a playlist that nourishes your body, mind and soul

Yoga pose – Lotus (or comfortable simple seated) sit bones on mat or cushion

Root (red) – Lord please ground me and root me. Thank you for walking with me everywhere I go, I pray that You keep my ways tethered to You at all times, never leave my side Lord. You are the way the truth and the life. Thank You for all the blessings of this day and thank You Jesus for being my very best friend.

Sexuality (orange) – Lord thank you for my sexuality and sensuality. Help me honour and respect this precious gift. Help me be mindful and sensitive to who I am in You and who You want me to be within my intimate relationship.

Desire (yellow) – Lord help me direct my energies wisely. Lord intersect my life where I need more of You and less of me and the world. Help me let go of my fear, doubts, anxieties and replace those with confidence of who I am in You. And help me be okay with who I am today as You refine me each and every day in your image.

Love (green) – Lord thank You for loving me! Thank you for showing me how to love and thank you for allowing me to be a conduit of Your love. Help lead me to places where I can be the light in the lives of others. Help me love and cherish myself despite my flaws. Help me love unconditionally without obligation or expectation. Help me love then love some more. Help me not to be afraid of love because in true love there is no fear.

Truth (blue) – Lord help me see the truth, hear the truth and speak Your truth. Help me find You in all that I see, do and say. Guard my words and help me say the right thing at the right time. Help me build others up. Might all that I say glorify Your Holy name.

Wisdom (indigo) – Lord You are most wise, I pray for Your knowledge, wisdom and Your understanding in each and every situation in my life. Lord I ask that You bring to light areas of my life that I need to lean into You more. Remind me constantly that Your will be done, not mine.

Protection (violet) – Lord keep me in Your protective custody. Keep all those that I love in Your protective custody.

Journal for 15-20 mins about things that came up for you during the meditation.

Q - Grounding Meditation

Activate and balance the root chakra:

Spray feet with eucalyptus essential oil (diluted for topical usage)

Rub cedarwood infused topical oil on feet.

Walk barefoot (if you can), find a shoreline, find a forest, find a mountain range, lay on the grass and watch the clouds, do your yoga practice outside, have a picnic – ultimately find a place that is outdoors and where you can appreciate all of his creations. Then pick a scripture that speaks to you and meditate on what it means for you today.

Here are a few suggested scriptures allowing you to root down so you can rise up:

Ephesians 3:16-19 The Voice

Father, out of Your honorable and glorious riches, strengthen Your people. Fill their souls with the power of Your Spirit so that through faith the Anointed One will reside in their hearts. May love be the rich soil where their lives take root. May it be the bedrock where their lives are founded so that together with all of Your people they will have the power to understand that the love of the Anointed is infinitely long, wide, high, and deep, surpassing everything anyone previously experienced. God, may Your fullness flood through their entire beings.

Jeremiah 17:7-8 The Voice

But blessed is the one who trusts in Me *alone*; the Eternal will be his confidence. He is like a tree planted by water, sending out its roots beside the stream. It does not fear the heat or even drought. Its leaves stay green and its fruit is dependable, *no matter what it faces.*

Colossians 2:6-7 The Voice

Now that you have welcomed the Anointed One, Jesus the Lord, into your lives, continue to journey with Him *and allow Him to shape your lives.* Let your roots grow down deeply in Him, and let Him build you up on a firm foundation. Be strong in the faith, just as you were taught, and always spill over with thankfulness.

Take time to journal your thoughts, describe what you seen, heard, smelled and touched, engage the senses. What resonated with your heart? What was the Lord speaking to you? What prayers could you develop from this experience?

R - Yoga Sequences

Visit anitastettner.com and book a private yoga session or try one of the online classes.

Gentle Flow Yoga (1 hour)
Description: 3-5 minutes scripture mediation, followed by a 15 min core warm up, leading into a 20 minute gentle flow with a 15 minute cool down gentle body, mind soul stretch.

Restorative Yoga (1 hour)
Description: 13-15 minute scripture meditation, followed by a gentle core warm up, leading into a sequence of restorative poses then concluding with a gentle final relaxing stretch.

Endurance Flow Yoga (50-55 minutes)
Description: 2-3 minute scripture meditation, followed by a 7-10 min core warm up, leading into a 30-35 minute endurance flow concluding with balance poses and gentle stretch.

Printed in the United States
By Bookmasters